Remote Controlled

Berry's World

© 1992 by NEA, Inc.

Remote Controlled

How TV Affects You and Your Family

Joe L. Wheeler

REVIEW AND HERALD® PUBLISHING ASSOCIATION
HAGERSTOWN, MD 21740

The author assumes full responsibility for the accuracy of all facts and quotations as cited in this book.

Texts credited to NEB are from *The New English Bible.* © The Delegates of the Oxford University Press and the Syndics of the Cambridge University Press 1961, 1970. Reprinted by permission.

Bible texts credited to Phillips are from J. B. Phillips: *The New Testament in Modern English,* Revised Edition. © J. B. Phillips 1958, 1960, 1972. Used by permission of Macmillan Publishing Co.

The author has tried his best to locate the copyright owners of every poem quoted in this book. If he has mistakenly given improper credit, please contact him immediately through the publisher.

This book was
Edited by Richard W. Coffen
Designed by Bill Kirstein
Cover art by Lee Cherry
Typeset: 11.5/13 Sabon

PRINTED IN U.S.A.

98 97 96 95 94 93   10 9 8 7 6 5 4 3 2 1

R & H Cataloging Service
Wheeler, Joe L   1936-
    Remote controlled.

    1. Television—Moral and religious aspects.
2. Television and children.   3. Television—Psychological aspects.   4. Television broadcasting—Psychological aspects.   5. Television broadcasting—Social aspects.   I. Title.
        306.485

ISBN 0-8280-0713-6

Dedicated to
Connie, who has helped me
so much with this manuscript,
and
our beloved fathers:
Lawrence Anthony Wheeler
and
Derwood Dwight Palmer

Contents

Preface

Everywhere we look today, people are concerned—concerned as never before in this nation's history.

Perhaps it is occurring in part because five centuries have now passed since Columbus landed on the shores of San Salvador.

Perhaps it is because we are in the countdown to the second millennium since Christ's life, death, and resurrection on this planet.

Perhaps it is because we are gradually sinking into the most severe economic depression since 1929.

Perhaps it is because ever-increasing crime and violence in our streets are robbing us of life as we once knew it.

Perhaps it is because the dramatic increase in those who prefer the homosexual or lesbian lifestyle is viewed as a major threat to the traditional American home by many in the heterosexual community.

Perhaps it is because we are belatedly realizing that we may no longer be the greatest nation anymore—clearly evident in terms of our swift flip-flop from greatest lender nation to greatest debtor nation . . . and our simultaneous surrender of our fiscal, economic, and industrial preeminence to Japan.

Perhaps it is because we now are beginning to realize just how flawed our highly touted education system really is. Graphic proof: decades of plunging ACT and SAT test scores.

Perhaps it is because we Americans have—as Hirsch and Bloom have already testified—lost our common heritage, no longer having anything in common but media and sports.

Perhaps it is because, without a Higher Power in our lives, we are increasingly finding life to be empty, purposeless, hollow, dead-end, and as tasteless as sawdust.

Perhaps it is because woman's belated rise to self-fulfillment has brought with it such an exorbitant price tag: the emptiness of lonely success, the emasculation of the male, the destruction of marriage and the cocoon we call "home," with all the attendant aftershocks of the defenseless children prematurely expelled from the home into an amoral wasteland.

Perhaps it is because, with the decline of reading, reason, and church attendance, coupled with the societal tilt toward the sensory and the occult, we are finding it difficult to reach any ideological bedrock, and are frightened as we feel society's foundations tottering under us.

Perhaps it is because the recent Los Angeles race riots graphically brought home to us the realization that the veneer separating civilization and savagery is far thinner than we had realized. Clearly the slightest break can result in undreamed-of violence, cruelty, death, destruction, mass theft—all juxtaposed against a background of powerless police and civic officials, highlighted by a raging inferno.

Perhaps it is because of the leadership of eight individuals (Dan and Marilyn Quayle, Tipper and Al Gore, Barbara and George Bush, Bill and Hillary Clinton) who challenged the media as have no other counterparts in American history. And both parties, instead of wrapping their campaigns in the flag of patriotism, wrapped them in family values.

Perhaps it is because we now realize that only a miracle can save our battered planet—that the world population explosion represents such a vast avalanche of impending doom that we are powerless to do much more than stare in a sort of frozen horror.

Perhaps it is because the new and peaceful world order we thought had arrived with the dismantling of the Berlin Wall and the iron curtain is proving to be anything but. Instead, we see the Balkanization of Europe all over again: each ethnic or religious subgroup attacking its neighbor. What once was Yugoslavia is today in chaos, practicing genocide on its own people, destroying historic and architectural treasures that had survived for millenniums. The euphoria of Vaclav Havel and Czechoslovakia lasting a mere two and a half years before disintegrating with Havel's sad walk out of Prague Castle. All over Europe the old Stalinist guard, masquerading in democracy's clothing, is sneaking back into power again. And the mere threat of tens of millions of hungry refugees flooding Western Europe from the east sends chills up the spines of Common Market members. And as a result, geography is changing faster than mapmakers can keep up with.

Perhaps it is because the media have so concentrated on the mistakes and frailties of those who govern us that we are in grave danger of losing faith in the democratic process itself. The huge wave of support for H. Ross Perot before he had so much as articulated who he was, what he stood for, or what he felt he could accomplish, if elected, is indicative of just how fragile our two-century-old system of government really is.

Perhaps it is because of a delayed reaction to the 75-year-old Cold War, during which time it was hard not to join the patriotic bandwagon which held that America represented God and Christian values, whereas Communism and Leninism represented the evil power. But what now? With Communism being proved morally and economically bankrupt and Russia again opening the doors to religion—which side is God on now?

Perhaps it is because we are just now feeling the first real repercussions from a fatherless society. For millenniums the family unit has remained constant with a divinely ordained father, mother, child structure. But now the father is either stepping or being pushed aside, and women are attempting the impossible: to be mother and father, caregiver and career woman, to provide tough love as well as soft and tender love, to protect from without and nurture from within. It remains to be seen whether this impossible state of affairs can be rectified before our society collapses in upon itself.

Perhaps it is because, as we have become more highly educated, we have also become more secular. This loss of faith in God, this abdication of fundamentals in favor of relativism, has brought with it an erosion both of our long-vaunted self-confidence and our sense of purpose, and it is contributing greatly to a general atmosphere of doubt and despair.

Perhaps it is because the media agents we blame for the current sad state of our affairs are themselves restless and unhappy with what they have degenerated to. Even Caliban can turn. It is indeed surprising to note the number of the so-called secular media who are themselves now warning against the very forces they unleashed upon us. Ironically, they now find themselves being savaged by their own pit bulls.

Perhaps it is because we—all of us—like the sorcerer's apprentice in Disney's *Fantasia*, have collectively and individually, by overt act as well as default, contributed to a society now being engulfed by tidal forces of our own making . . . and like Mickey Mouse as he was being sucked into oblivion by his own whirlpool, we yearn for the Master to part the waters and save us from ourselves.

Regardless of whether some of these—or all of these—reasons
are at the root of our concern, the reality is this: Never before has
concern been greater. Without such a widespread outcry this book
would never have been written.

What We Have Become

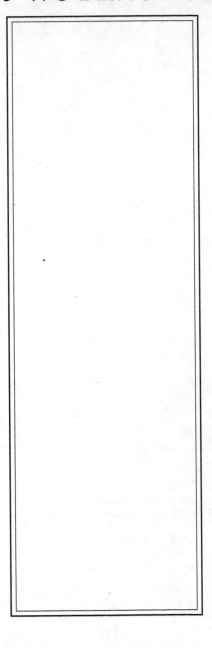

♦

CHAPTER 1

Marks on the Soul

We just don't understand where it was that we lost Natasha. We gave her everything! We even sacrificed and gave up things we personally wanted very much so that she could have the best diet (both as an infant and as a child), the best medical and dental care, the best clothes and accessories, the best tutoring and schooling—even an Ivy League college. She has never, to our knowledge, gone without anything money could buy that she really wanted.

As a preschooler, we made sure she had baby-sitters with the highest credentials. We gave orders that she was to be kept home so that she would not play with non-Christian children. How fortunate that we had TV sets all over the house so that she always had something to do. And we were the first in our block to buy a VCR. Throughout the years, we have built up for her an enormous library of movies on video—in fact, her friends tell her they know of no one who has a bigger collection.

In order to keep her from being bored, the TV set or VCR has always been on in our house, from the moment we get up until we retire at night. She learned so much about life from Sesame Street, Mr. Rogers, sitcoms, talk shows, the soaps, movies, and commercials. We never had to tell her the facts of life! Why, she was already asking for bras when she was only 4!

Lately, however, she has begun listening to the radio and her Walkman more, as well as the latest hits on MTV. Like her friends, she knows all the lyrics. It's amazing, the memory of that girl. She never seems to study, yet she still pulls respectable grades—not the highest, but enough to keep her off scholastic probation.

She used to go to church with us but lost interest in it years ago—said it was "bor-ing!" Recently we've noticed some lifestyle changes we don't approve of: some nights she comes home drunk in the wee hours of the morning; she has smoked ever since she was 13—in spite of our telling her it can cut her life short; after we found some suspicious-looking needles in her bathroom she admitted to doing drugs "once in a while"; and she and her current significant other are planning to move in together next week.

Somewhere along the way we must have failed, because our

values are not her values and our God is not hers either. When we speak with her about these things, she just laughs in that flippant way she has and walks out of the room. After all that we have done for Natasha, our wishes mean absolutely nothing to her!

Please tell us, where did we go wrong?

♦ ♦ ♦

Long before the advent of television, American poet Walt Whitman wrote:

"It was Halloween week, and the electronic jack-o'-lantern was casting a decidedly weird spell. On NBC, the mini-series Favorite Son showed sadomasochistic bondage, near-explicit masturbation and a dog lapping up the blood of a murder victim. On ABC, a made-for-TV movie focused on a psychotic father setting fire to his sleeping son. On Fox Television's The Reporters, the big story was about an airline pilot who disposed of his wife by shoving her body through a wood-chipping machine. The talk shows, too, were doing their bit. Morton Downey, Jr., hosted a gaggle of strippers while Sally Jessy Raphael chatted with some lesbian marriage partners. Geraldo Rivera? Pretty much a standard week's performance: encounters with former prostitutes and female boxers, topped off with a titillating exposé of sexual abuse by doctors" ("Trash TV," Newsweek, Nov. 14, 1988).

> "There was a child went forth every day,
>   And the first object he look'd upon,
>   that object he became,
>   And that object became part of him."

How true it is that each of us is the sum total of what we have been exposed to. Certainly we media and computer sophisticates of the 1990s ought to recognize this great truth: garbage in, garbage out. But how strange that we know this fact of life abstractly yet fail to act upon it where the most crucial responsibility the Lord entrusts to us mortals is concerned: raising our children. We rationalize and temporize by saying, "Well, surely just one little program couldn't hurt Billy *that* much." And then: "That last one really wasn't as bad as I feared it might be. Sure, it's OK for Billy to watch that program tonight."

And it proves to be downhill from there, for once principle is compromised, there ceases to be an ethical base for future decisions.

In this vein no more powerful statement on the subject has ever been made than the following by C. S. Lewis in his monumental book *Mere Christianity*: "Every time you make a choice you are turning the central part of you, the part of you that chooses, into something a little different from what it was before. And taking your life as a whole, with all your innumerable choices, all your life long you are slowly turning this central thing either into a heavenly creature or into a hellish creature" (p. 72).

Each of these acts, these decisions, these determinations, has an effect both upon us and upon those whom our action affects. Lewis likens each to a mark on the soul, on what he labels the "central self which no one sees in this life but which each of us will have to endure—or enjoy—forever" (*ibid.*).

He goes on to note that, singly, these marks appear not to have much of an effect, but over time they tend to cluster, gradually becoming habits. And habits crystallize into character. And character determines one's eternal destiny.

CHAPTER 2

A World That Scares Me

Looking back at my childhood, I am convinced that I was lucky. In that TV-less environment I was able to mature at nature's gradual pace. I was able to dream, for I was given a great gift: quietness, which is so often denied today's children. It was during those far-off days that I learned to appreciate solitude and the opportunity to commune with my inner self.

Oh, how I loved for Mother to read out loud to us: to recite great poetry and tell moving stories by the hour! I was barely 5 when I discovered the magic of words on a printed page. I would follow my long-suffering mother—who was home for me all during my childhood and adolescence—reading book after book to her out loud in my high childish voice. And never once did she dampen my sense of wonder!

Many years later, my son and then my daughter were born into a far different world. Not long after Greg's birth, we bought our first television set—the weekend of President John F. Kennedy's assassination. Like thousands of other Christians, we bought that TV set with the best of intentions. We intended to control it. Belatedly, we realized that the small gray-green screen was altering the very fabric of our lives. We started out being extremely selective, ever so gradually widening the list of acceptable watching fare until we suddenly realized that we were endangering our son's spiritual and ethical well-being, to say nothing of our own.

Alexander Pope captured the process well in his immortal epigram:

> "Vice is a monster of so frightful mien,
> As to be hated needs but to be seen;
> Yet seen too oft, familiar with her face,
> We first endure, then pity, then embrace."

So many, like us, buy that first TV set, that first VCR, with the best of intentions. We will watch the news and documentaries and educational, literary, inspirational, and nature-related programming only. But, almost inevitably, control gradually slips. Each additional program or video looks so innocent—and certainly no more evil than its predecessor. Thus the observing family can descend from purity to blue language and pornography without ever realizing that repeated exposures to the medium has blurred ever so gradually the lines of distinction between good and evil in our now-unreliable control towers.

Few of us have really stopped to speculate much about what the mind, heart, and soul really are. As we noted earlier, we become what we are continually exposed to. Every experience of life is recorded by the mind's camera lens on archival tape, there to wait patiently until called for. All the dialogue with brother, sister, mother, father, teacher, minister, sweetheart, friend; all the books and magazines read; all the television programs, videos, and movies watched; all the lyrics on the radio and Walkman listened to; all the concerts, plays, and programs attended; all the school and church instruction given; all the letters written and received; all the places traveled to and scenes observed along the way—*all* is faithfully recorded by the mind and computerized for future reference. If you doubt this, listen to an old person who has somehow been able to discover in his or her archives vivid videos of childhood three quarters of a century before. It is a bit dusty because of nonuse—but it is there.

"In the tissues of your mind are recorded and stored billions upon billions of memories, habits, instincts, abilities, desires and hopes and fears and patterns and tinctures and sounds and inconceivably delicate calculations and brutishly crude urgencies, the sound of a whisper heard 30 years ago, . . . the delight never experienced but incessantly imagined, the complex structure of stresses in a bridge, the exact pressure of a single finger on a single string, the development of ten thousand different games of chess, the precise curve of a lip, a hill, an equation, or a flying ball, tones and shades and glooms and raptures, the faces of countless strangers, the scent of one's garden, prayers, inventions, poems, jokes, tunes, sums, problems unsolved, victories long past, the fear of hell and the love of God, the vision of a blade of grass and the vision of the sky filled with stars" (Gilbert Highet, **Man's Unconquerable Mind**).

Perhaps the most significant interview of Roland Hegstad's lifetime was chronicled in his powerful little book *Mind Manipulators:*

"One of the most fascinating discoveries of scientists charting the human mind has been the discovery of neuron circuits related to memory in our temporal lobes. . . . Recently I spent several hours talking with Dr. Wilder Penfield, former director of the world-famous Montreal Neurological Institute [later, Penfield was Professor of Neurophysiology at McGill University]. It was studies by Dr. Penfield that revealed this file of memories reaching back to earliest childhood. By using a probe that delivered an electronic shock to the brain tissue, Dr. Penfield triggered vivid recall of long-forgotten events. It was, he said, 'as though a strip of cinema film had been set in motion within the brain.'

"Dr. Penfield told me of operating on a young woman suffering from epilepsy. When he stimulated a point on the surface of her cortex she heard an orchestra playing. In surprise she asked whether music was being piped into the operating room. When Dr. Penfield turned off the electric probe the music stopped. Every time the current was turned on, and he moved the needle to the same spot, the orchestra started up again, and the woman listened to it, at its original tempo, from verse to chorus, just as she had heard it years before. She even re-experienced the thrill of emotion she had felt while sitting in the theater. The whole performance had been indelibly inscribed on microscopic cells of her mind.

"The significant fact we should note here is that events of which we have no conscious recall are nevertheless printed—as if on a cinema film—within our mind. Every television program, every radio drama, every billboard message, every advertisement, every book and magazine read, every person scrutinized, every suspicion harbored, every word spoken—it's all there. And those unconscious memories—the sum total of all that we have put into our mind—make up the kind of person we are today and will be tomorrow" (Hegstad, *Mind Manipulators,* pp. 13, 14).

It is indeed one of the wonders of God's universe how this vast living library of videotape translates into day-to-day behavior. As babies we were, except for inherited tendencies, virtually unprogrammed. However, as the years pass, we become more and more the prisoners of our library. We find it increasingly difficult to deviate from what we are and have been in the past. As long as we live, breathe, and retain control, the opportunity to change will exist—but it is dependent on what new videos are being cataloged and wired into our mainframe each day, or, as C. S. Lewis would put it, on the marks that continue to be made on our souls.

Ever since reading these two powerful statements by Dr. Penfield and Dr. James, I have found myself being even more careful about what I watch. I now find myself first posing the question Is this something I want to poison my memory with for the rest of my life?

All this is even more frightening in that what comes to us via nonprint media bypasses the censors of our minds. Dr. Eric Peper stated the

"The hell to be endured hereafter, of which theology tells, is no worse than the hell we make for ourselves in this world by habitually fashioning our characters in the wrong way. Could the young but realize how soon they will become mere walking bundles of habits, they would give more heed to their conduct while in the plastic state. We are spinning our own fates, good or evil, and never to be undone. Every smallest stroke of virtue or of vice leaves its never so little scar. The drunken Rip Van Winkle, in Jefferson's play, excuses himself for every fresh dereliction by saying, 'I won't count this time!' Well! he may not count it, and a kind Heaven may not count it; but it is being counted none the less. Down among his nerve-cells and fibres the molecules are counting it, registering and storing it up to be used against him when the next temptation comes. Nothing we ever do is, in strict scientific literalness, wiped out" (William James, **The Principles of Psychology,** p. 83).

problem this way: "The horror of television is that the information goes in, but we don't react to it. It goes directly into our memory pool—later we react to it but we don't know what we are reacting to. We have trained ourselves not to react, but later on we do things without knowing why, or even where the impulse came to us" (quoted in Jerry Mander's book, *Four Arguments for the Elimination of Television*).

Truly this is a frightening age in which to bring up a child. Prior to the early sixties, it remained possible for parents to monitor to a major extent the avenues to their child's mind, heart, and soul. Television dramatically changed that, for it represents an unlocked door into virtually every home in the nation. As long as parents remained the key programmers of their child's early years, a normal childhood remained possible, but when they permitted an alien presence to enter their homes, an alien over which they had no control, an alien which could speak at the touch of a knob with or without adult supervision—that act changed everything.

Educators tell us that half of what we learn in a lifetime we learn before we even enter the first grade. It is consumed in torrents. Never again in the child's life will knowledge be so eagerly sought . . . or learned and assimilated at such breakneck speed. The most complex languages on earth can be quickly mastered, one after another, during these first magic years.

During these critical early years the sails are being set for life. Patterns once established will be very difficult to change later on. Concepts of what is right and what is wrong are clearly established during these preschool years, and fortunate is the child who enters first grade with moral and ethical shafts firmly anchored on Christ and the Mosaic code.

Tragically, in respect to the welfare of the child, running parallel to the media's intrusion into our homes has been the growth of two-paycheck households. No longer is mother at home with the preschooler. Instead, the child is farmed out to baby-sitters or child-care centers—few of which are staffed with deeply committed Christians who take seriously their awesome responsibility to help instill a Christian philosophy of life and assist in developing Christ-centered patterns of behavior.

Questions come at such breakneck speed and in such an unrelenting stream that even parents are likely to reach circuit overloads. How well I remember one day when my own son Greg responded to his frustrated father's

"It does not matter how small the sins are provided that their cumulative effect is to edge the man away from the Light and out into the Nothing. Murder is no better than cards if cards can do the trick. Indeed, the safest road to Hell is the gradual one— the gentle slope, soft underfoot, without sudden turnings, without milestones, without signposts" (C. S. Lewis, The Screwtape Letters, pp. 61, 62).

plea to leave him in peace—after his 101st consecutive question— with a retort none of the family has ever forgotten: "Questions help me know things!"

But when parents abdicate the responsibility to be there for the child during the crucial years, the damage to the mind, heart, and soul are likely to be irreparable. Not many hired substitutes will have either the patience or the time to nurture tenderly the growth of this delicate flower so that its petals are not bruised. All too often the TV or the VCR will represent an easy way to sidetrack such an unwelcome responsibility. And what will be the philosophy of life instilled by this flickering blue parent? A number of years ago, when industry broadcasting standards were considerably higher than they are now, *Newsweek* editors answered that question in an illuminating cover article.

"His first polysyllabic utterance was 'Bradybunch.' He learned to spell Sugar Smacks before his own name. He has seen Monte Carlo, witnessed a cocaine bust in Harlem, and already has full-color fantasies involving Farrah Fawcett-Majors. Recently he tried to karate-chop his younger sister after she broke his Six Million Dollar Man bionic transport station. (She retaliated by bashing him with her Cher doll.) His nursery school teacher reports that he is passive, noncreative, unresponsive to instruction, bored during play periods, and possessed of an almost nonexistent attention span—in short, very much like his classmates. Next fall, he will officially reach the age of reason and begin his formal education. His parents are beginning to discuss their apprehensions—when they are not too busy watching television" ("What TV Does to Kids," Feb. 21, 1977).

Since 1977 what is permitted on television has been so expanded that today apparently nothing is off-limits to industry hucksters as they battle for ratings. And the impact on the child of this continual cannonading of the soul? Truths and realities that even adults find difficult to handle are beamed directly to adolescents and children who are totally unprepared to handle such incendiary material. As a result, who knows how many million children and youth have had their internal moral, spiritual, and ethical control centers short-circuited by the premature dazzling of adult realities—followed by fleeing these unfaceable specters into dead-end alleys of liquor, drugs, indiscriminate sex, and suicide.

Thus it is that television all too often spawns cynical, world-weary, jaded, sensual, perverted, twisted children who are deprived of the needed illusions of childhood and youth by the "reality" of televised experience, and they are catapulted into visual adulthood years before they can handle that level of circuit overload.

It seems oddly ironic that parents who would view as unthinkable stacking their coffee tables and shelves with books that graphically illustrate, in living color, every imaginable form of perversion would pay no attention at all to the far more vivid portrayals of these same acts on their home TV sets! Furthermore, those who have carefully analyzed current television fare declare that the values commonly portrayed (other than a handful of striking exceptions, such as *The Cosby Show*) are almost totally antithetical to those that Christians believe in. Where in television are children likely to find traditional role models that are in harmony with the Christian way of life?

"Truth must dazzle gradually Or every man be blind" (Emily Dickinson).

Why should it surprise us, then, that our young people see nothing wrong in casually walking away from a spouse and family when the televised norm is live-in lover rather than marriage for life? When God is a swearword, when honesty is for naive fools, when hard work is for the stupid, when fidelity is but a change of pace, when unselfish caring is featured in *Believe It or Not*—why should we be surprised that our youth are walking away from God and the church?

"How old should I be before I marry for the first time?"

SIDEGLANCES reprinted by permission of NEA, Inc.

CHAPTER 3

The Child Is Father of the Man

In Scripture we are told that for everything there is a season, a divinely ordained time for the stages of our lives. If the preschool home cocoon is not broken prematurely, the child ought to reach the age of 6 with God's greatest gift, the sense of wonder, intact.

Wordsworth was correct when he declared that the child is father of the man. What the child is is what the man or woman will become. Far too often we parents forget how plastic are the minds, hearts, and souls of our children—rather, we tend to look upon them as static products. We stereotype them by our own early impressions and tend to lock them into these behavioral straitjackets. We forget that our children are in a state of becoming, that they are capable of dramatic change and growth. Let's face it, we are with them too much. If we are away from them for a few weeks, we quickly notice changes; but, with them almost constantly, we fail to notice these gradations and hence mistakenly assume no changes are taking place.

As we all know, we adults too are continually changing, altering our behavior from what we are today to what we are becoming, and with children the potential for change is greater— far greater. Permit me a sports analogy: We often see football game instant replays, with the action, which had previously been so rapid that we had a hard time following it, slowed down so we could observe the sequence of events. I am suggesting that parents should slow down the speed of their interaction with their children. Remember that, to a child, all life is now—tomorrow seems an eternity away, and yesterday is only a blur. For the child the past has not yet come into focus as a reality and frame of reference.

◆ ◆ ◆

Three Days With a 2-Year-Old

I had forgotten—or maybe I had just mercifully blotted it out of my conscious memory—just what it was like to have a 2-year-old in the house, ricocheting at top speed within four walls. I had forgotten how long it takes to eat a meal when parents have to get up every few seconds to rescue an endangered object from the child or the child from a dangerous object or situation. I had for-

"My heart leaps up when I behold
A rainbow in the sky;
So was it when my life began;
So is it now that I am a man;
So be it when I shall grow old,
Or let me die!
The child is father of the Man;
And I could wish my days to be
Bound each to each by natural
piety" (Wordsworth).

gotten how different a child-proof house is from one which isn't. I had forgotten how all-consuming, how time-devouring, how autocratic and utterly self-centered, a small child is. I had forgotten how the questions are machine-gunned at you in such an unceasing fusillade that the whole fabric of the day appears to be nothing more than a seamless garment of question and answer interwoven with don't do this and don't you dare do that cross-stitching. And I had forgotten that rather sad but wonderfully therapeutic feeling that washes over you when the unguided missile finally drops off to sleep and you awake to the quietness of a cease-fire after a major battle—only *then* being able to accomplish anything else but keep the child alive and satisfied. Most of all, I had forgotten just how voracious was the 2-year-old appetite for the world, knowledge, and growth.

And I couldn't help but ruefully look back at the ever so glib advice I had shoveled out to the mothers of preschool children, who were valiantly trying to complete a college degree while remaining effective mothers—and belatedly I turned beet red.

After the child and his parents had boarded the plane for California and we returned to a suddenly serene home, with the worst enemy our fragile bric-a-brac had being Pandora the Himalayan feline (always on a strict regimen of 15 seconds of vigorous activity offset by 23 hours, 59 minutes, and 45 seconds of deep sleep, half-deep sleep, and dozing), I suddenly realized how glad I was that I had written this book. Glad because perhaps these feeble words of mine might perhaps make it possible for other Alexes in hectic America to preserve their sense of wonder through childhood, adolescence, youth, and the rest of their lives—that God-given sense of wonder which flowered so briefly in our house New Year's weekend, 1993.

◆ ◆ ◆

You are busy—to the child, you are always busy—and your child asks permission to watch TV. You agree . . . but today I am asking that you drop everything else and watch too, but with a major difference: Pretend that you too are an innocent and idealistic 3-year-old, drunk with the beauty of the "rainbow in the sky." Then you turn on the set, and what do you see? In graphic riveting color, you see every perversion and evil imaginable, and—like a mother in one of my adult evening classes did not long ago—you will be appalled! All *that* is being programmed into the computer memory banks of your children, and from those memory banks your children will conceptualize the values they will live by for the rest of their lives.

Wilder Penfield likens the brain to an iceberg. The tip (less than 10 percent of what we have been exposed to) has to do with our conscious memory, containing the data we consider most important and wish to access frequently. But beneath the conscious mind is the unconscious, containing 90 percent of our memories. These are not as easily recalled to the conscious . . . but they are there, and, when triggered by the right impulse, will surface. Dr. Penfield concludes that "nothing is ever really forgotten" (Roland Hegstad, *Mind Manipulators*).

Richard Fredericks has observed that "character is never formed in a crisis—it is only revealed in a crisis. As

"Each day is a thread woven into the tapestry of life, and we have the power to choose the colors" (Author Unknown).

each teenager begins to establish his own adult identity, meaningful relationships, and a personal value system, he will largely be a self-fulfilling prophecy of whatever his mind has fed on in all his early years. He will handle new experiences based on his past experiences—or lack of them" (Richard Fredericks, "Television and the Christian Family," unpublished study, Andrews University, Berrien Springs, Michigan, 1981).

"But," you may retort, "my children need to see both good and

evil so they can make up their own minds about values. I'm not going to force *my* children into any mold!" What you are ignoring is that children do not yet have the ability to differentiate between what is good and what is evil, between what will help or what will hurt. Psychologists tell us that not until their teens do children fully recognize the difference between reality and unreality.

That truth was vividly brought home to me a number of years ago. I had just read the previous evening Aldous Huxley's warning about the powers held by the mass media in contemporary society. He stated that one of the most dangerous aspects of screen imagery is that a child does not know how to differentiate between reality and unreality on the screen.

I read this, and it registered—vaguely. The following evening my 4-year-old boy came racing into the room where I was studying, screaming at me to come into the other room immediately. As I strode into the room where he had been eyeing a

Western show, he shouted: "Daddy, that man is going to *kill* that man!" To him that was reality on the screen. Ever since then I have carefully policed the screen when small children are within viewing distance. All of us have read news stories about children who murder and then almost disintegrate in grief when they discover that the victim is not going to get up and appear later, the way they do on TV (they see the same actor who was killed on one show appear safe and sound on another).

Let's say your 2-year-old son toddles over toward the red-hot stove that he sees lighting up the dark kitchen. Mesmerized, he reaches up to feel this wonderful thing. Do you let him find out for himself, as his flesh fries on that burner? Certainly not! You know the consequences of such an act, and you warn your child to stop.

As heartless as it may sound, it would be better for you to permit your child to burn his hand so that it could never be used again than it would be to permit him to have his moral control center programmed by the dark power. There is more than ample opportunity for children to observe evil without our introducing it ourselves. In our society children will be deluged with it, and it will take all the bailing out that parents, family, ministers, and educators can do just to keep the frail ship afloat. If we permit evil to enter our children's minds through television in our homes, we become an accessory to the crime of corrupting an innocent mind. We could have controlled access to the most powerful communicating device ever invented . . . until our children were able to handle the material in their maturity.

Humorist Erma Bombeck sometimes gets concerned enough about a social issue to forsake humor and get serious. In one column she noted the mind-numbing TV exposure the average high school graduate has been exposed to: "Forget the 22,836 sitcoms and the 350,000 commercials he will have witnessed. The main concern is, what else is he getting out of worshiping at the shrine of prime time for 18,000 hours? [Currently, 22,000 hours.]

"A loss of innocence, for one. . . .

"The odds are good that a role model will emerge from this little tube, along with values that will have a greater effect on his life than those of his parents" ("Things You Learn by Watching TV," Fort Worth *Star-Telegram*, Dec. 13, 1981).

Prior to the invention of television, the school picked up where the home left off, and both continued the educational process, in step, so that children were not confronted with issues before it was time. All that was possible with the print media. Joshua Meyrowitz noted that "in print media, the child learns the secrets of the adult world gradually through a system of graded texts and carefully screened messages of parents and teachers. . . . TV undermines schools . . . It gives them [children] knowledge too soon" ("Professor Claims TV Destroyed Childhood Concept," Cleburne, Texas, *Times-Review*, Aug. 13, 1982).

Neil Postman, New York University professor and one of television's most eminent scholars, warned that television "eliminates many of the important ways we distinguish between children and adults. For example, one of the main differences between an adult and a child is that the adult knows about certain facts of life — its mysteries, its contradictions, its violence, its tragedies — that are not considered suitable for children to know, or even accessible to children. What television does is to bring the whole culture out of the closet, because programs need a constant supply of novel information [talk shows, for instance]. In its quest for new and sensational ventures to hold its audience, *TV must tap every existing taboo in our culture:* homosexuality, incest, divorce, promiscuity, cor-

> *"If there is no clear concept of what it means to be an adult, there can be no concept of what it means to be a child"* (Neil Postman, *"TV's 'Disastrous' Impact on Children,"* **U.S. News & World Report, Jan. 19, 1981).**

ruption, adultery, and terrible displays of violence and sadism. As a consequence, these things become as familiar to the young as they are to adults" ("TV's 'Disastrous' Impact on Children," *U.S. News & World Report*, Jan. 19, 1981; italics supplied).

In this respect, Postman sadly noted that some of the nation's highest paid models are 12- to 13-year-old girls who are presented as sexually enticing adults. Thus, it gets harder and harder to find children being portrayed as children. Even the commercials play this up: "Which is the mother, which is the daughter?"

But Postman was not through: "Television relentlessly undermines most of its characters' capacities to be adult, to say no and mean it, to live with uncertainty. Viewers are encouraged to remain immature, with no sense of belonging, no capacity for lasting relationships, no respect for limits, no grasp of the future. . . . In a culture that is actively encouraging 9-year-olds to be 29-year-olds, I think parents have to work extra hard to preserve their children's childhood" *(ibid.).*

"Observe, for example, how television treats religion. On our nighttime fare, religious figures are readily parodied. Catholics are portrayed as closed-minded bigots with the morals of Torquemada; fundamentalist Protestants are, as one show described them, 'Bible-thumpin' hayseeds.' A review of every prime-time television show from the '89-90 and '90-91 seasons shows that only one series (Thirtysomething) ever depicted religious institutions in a positive light. Every other program was neutral or negative toward religion" (L. Brent Bozell III, "Peddlers of Smut," Washington Post, Feb. 23, 1993).

When asked if it was really important to preserve a concept of childhood, Prof. Postman responded: "Yes. The invention of childhood was one of the most humane inventions of the Renaissance. What it did was to make it a cultural principle that we had to nurture and protect children. It promoted ideas through society that are important, such as curiosity and malleability and innocence and a sense of continuity and re-creation. These are qualities that we've come to associate with childhood that are necessary prerequisites for developing into mature adulthood" *(ibid.).*

But just what can we do to help provide such a protected childhood? Don Oldenburg, in a 1988 column, devoted a great deal of space to the thoughts and convictions of the Rabbi Neil Kurshan, of Huntington, New York: "Identifying himself as a liberal theologian who believes in the 'power and authority of religion to reinforce values in the family,' Kurshan says the most important goal parents can have for their children is that they grow up to be kind and moral.

"The extended family always provided a foundation of values from two or three generations to the next. But the extended family often exists only through infrequent visits and long-distance telephone calls."

Where educators once reinforced common values, according to Kurshan, today's teachers and administrators generally tiptoe around teaching moral values so as not to ask for trouble from public factions who object. Concerning this vacuum, Kurshan warns, "When we begin to doubt the absolute goodness of God, and even His very existence, we are left with only ourselves as the final arbiters of morality."

And when that happens, what do we get? "Relativity of values is the reigning ideology." And Kurshan likened that to "building a condo on quicksand."

Kurshan postulates that "with no firm priorities in values, children become confused and anxious over the array of alternatives. If everything is of equal worth, that process of maturation becomes difficult. . . . When a consensus of values breaks down in communities, you get safe philosophies that only muddle the situation. Children need clearly defined values and standards."

Kurshan concludes with this ringing statement: "Parents are the best and perhaps only hope for reestablishing common ethical and moral grounds" (cited in Don Oldenburg, "Kids and Morals in a Me-First World," Washington *Post*, Mar. 25, 1988).

CHAPTER 4

❖

Teen Viewers and a Darker Sound of Music

Where teenagers are concerned, a whole new set of TV-related variables comes into play. According to the Reading in America study, teenagers continue to do poorly in standardized testing. "They do not seem to be able to catch implications in reading, make predictions, form generalizations, reach conclusions, make comparisons, form judgments, or create new ideas . . . without significant difficulty" (National Assessment of Educational Progress, Denver, 1978).

Furthermore, according to Marie Winn, as a group they tend to reject reason and intellectual activity in favor of the nonlogical, unsequential, disconnected, and the absolute primacy of feeling over thinking. Not surprisingly, they are heavy users of drugs, both legal and illegal, and are prone to sensation - highs rather than being willing to work for eventual success. They are disciples of instant gratification, spectators rather than participants.

"We're tired, often more from boredom than exertion, old without being wise, worldly not from seeing the world but from watching it on television" (Joyce Maynard, Looking Back, p. 6).

As to why the tendency to gravitate to hard drugs or alcohol, Richard Fredericks is convinced that a key reason is that the heavy TV watchers have already been conditioned to expect vivid and fast imagery by the media, yet living as they do vicariously, they have almost no self-identity, consequently they feel empty within. They are bored, and all their relationships are shallow ones. Hence they are ripe for hard drugs, which—like TV—offer sensation without having to work for it.

Because of the short attention spans of frequent viewers, more and more the televised conversations are telescoped—not so much conversations as exchanges—and usually the feeble plot is carried along by the action. Fredericks notes that "conflict on TV is resolved by action, not by normal discussion involving extended explanations and empathetic listening"—still another reason why frequent viewers are often unable to communicate well anymore!

As to why suicide is now such a major killer, psychiatrists maintain that television leads children to expect quick answers to every situation and undermines their ability to tolerate frustration. Programs present serious problems and then solve them in one half hour. Life just doesn't work that way (Jerry Mander, *Four Arguments for the Elimination of Television*).

"Life is presented as a supercharged adventure, packed with excitement in which all frustrations are eliminated in short order. Things such as anxiety, insecurity, lingering illnesses, a poor complexion, repeated failure, or a physical handicap are unheard-of. As a result, the TV generation copes poorly with life's real frustrations and long-term problems. The TV-nurtured child comes of age and suddenly there is competition, tough homework, or dating problems, and they are not psychologically equipped to ride it out. So they drop out, drug out, run out, or check out—literally" (Richard Fredericks, "Television and the Christian Family," unpublished study, Andrews University, 1981).

That approximately two thirds of our marriages end in divorce should not surprise us, because noncommitment is the hallmark of TV watchers. And on the tube, no one deals for long with any one problem. Fredericks, in the hard-hitting summation to his teen study, puts it this way: "By offering more excitement every 30 minutes than most people experience in a lifetime; by modeling short, intense conversations loaded with drama and emotion; by promising quick answers to every problem; and by refusing to show the tragic consequences of its idealized lifestyle, television is programming teenagers for boredom, insecurity, and failure. And at the same time it denies the reality of the need to cope, and the skills to cope with" ("Television and the Christian Family").

Lest we feel that by controlling TV we have solved our problems, let me stir into the mix radio, MTV, and the popular music scene. I first became aware of changing realities, in this respect, several years ago when I surveyed my college freshmen about their media and reading habits. What jolted me was the discovery that their TV viewing had dropped from 30 hours a week to about 20. Good news! But they were watching more and more videos, frequently attending the cinema and live concerts, and—

most significant of all—were listening to about 50 hours a week of radio, cassettes, CDs, and MTV. In fact, rarely (except when it is impossible or not in order) were they *not* listening. More and more they would come to class wearing earphones, hoping I'd let them listen to their music rather than me!

Our students find it strangely difficult to memorize anything remotely tied to their schoolwork, yet paradox-

> *"Swans sing before they die—*
> *'Twere no bad thing*
> *Should certain persons die*
> *Before they sing" (Coleridge).*

ically they appear to know all the lyrics to all the Top 40 hits! Rarely will I find an adolescent, teenager, or young adult who won't be able to repeat instantly the lyrics to any popular tune on MTV or on radio. At 50 hours a week, that's 2,600 hours a year, or 26,000 hours during a 10-year period—twice as many hours as they will have spent in the classroom during elementary and high school years, and five times the number of hours they will have spent in college classrooms!

But if all they were doing was listening to music, there wouldn't be much of a problem. The problem is that precious few of these lyrics reinforce in any way, shape, or form the principles that Christians try to live by. Rather, the values portrayed are diametrically opposed to the tenets we have tried to teach them.

Even the academic world is becoming concerned. In a 1991 article in *Chronicle of Higher Education*, Scott Heller reported on the findings of Carl A. Raschke, a professor at the University of Denver. Dr. Raschke, in his recent book *Painted Black*, describes the spreading epidemic of satanist-related mayhem, including drug killings, hate crimes, and adolescent suicides. As is true with a number of other media scholars, he views the 1960s as a watershed turning away from traditional Judeo-Christian values toward antithetical ones.

He lashes out at heavy metal music, labeling it "full of dangerous and violent messages," and satanism as "the darkening of the counterculture . . . the black side of what happened in the sixties" *(ibid.).*

Columnist Donna Britt, responding to *Vanity Fair*'s August 1992 cover of Demi Moore posing nude but painted all over as if clothes were actually being worn—but transparent so that clearly they weren't—as well as her earlier pregnant nude cover, declared that the purveyors, participants, and gullible buyers alike evidenced abysmal taste.

" 'Satanism is terrorism,' Carl A. Raschke writes in Painted Black. 'It is the gestation of a permanent terrorist subculture in America that will bring the random violence and political intrigues of the Old World at last to the New' " (Scott Heller, "Entrepreneur of the Core Curriculum Fights the Devil on the Side," Chronicle of Higher Education, Jan. 9, 1991).

In this culture of hype, she noted, people will "literally say and do anything—*anything*—to get some attention. To sell to us." It used to be, she ruefully observed, that such shocking evidences of poor taste occurred only randomly—but now "the act of shocking, merely for its cash-generating value, has become mainstream. Everybody is doing it. . . . That is why in *Basic Instinct*, director Paul Verhoeven treated viewers to four photos of little kids with their throats slashed when one would have made the point. And *twice* showed Sharon Stone flashing what some still quaintly regard as her privates to a room full of cops. . . . It's why Ice-T, N.W.A, and Luther Campbell say such vile things in their albums. . . . It's why Madonna played 'lesbian' kissy face with Sandra Bernhard on a talk show, groveled in her slip before a black Jesus in the *Like a Prayer* video, and faked masturbation in her hyped-beyond-comprehension concert tour."

Britt followed up these incidents with other examples of media icons pandering to our society's basest instincts: including the obscene videos, the rock concerts that degenerate into orgies, and concluded with these sad lines:

" 'It's all related,' my friend says. 'When there's a sickness in society, the oppressed and the young get it worse. . . . Our culture is very sick. But it sure does sell' " (Donna Britt, "We Pay a High Price for Our Cheap Trends," Washington *Post*, July 24, 1992).

MTV, of course, reinforces the meaning of lyrics with sophisticated choreography, thus the visual is added to the aural, multiplying the effects upon the mind and soul of the listener.

And we professed Christians have hardly lifted a finger!

CHAPTER 5

Creativity and the Mind

When your child was born, what did you look for first? Yes, to see if the child was perfect physically . . . and mentally. What a joy to know that your biological link to immortality was whole.

Later on, as your child entered the world of school, you had a different worry: that somehow your child might fail to make the most of this opportunity and instead grow at a slower rate than classmates. Especially were you concerned with the development of those two crucial skills—reading and writing. At a much later date, you watched, deeply concerned, to see if the grown child's mind was adequate to meet the demands of adult life.

More and more often children are failing to live up to early expectations, and there is overwhelming evidence that television is the culprit in most of these cases. Studies reveal that about 97 percent of very small children are creative, but by the time those same children graduate from high school, the ratio will have flip-flopped, with 2 to 3 percent remaining creative!

For three decades now, ACT and SAT verbal test scores have been plummeting. Today one in every three Americans is functionally illiterate. Your Johnny comes home from school with a note from the teacher. In it the teacher tells you that your son finds it extremely difficult to write, and also appears to be a slow, unmotivated reader.

The breakdown in the ability to communicate on the written level is no laughing matter. It has become a national crisis. Some years ago, in a *Newsweek* cover story titled "Why Johnny Can't Write," Merrill Shiels (coordinator of the research project) observed: "There is no question in the minds of educators that a student who cannot read with true comprehension will never learn to write well. 'Writing is, after all, book-talk,' says Dr. Ramon Veal [of the University of Georgia]. . . . 'You learn book-talk only by reading' " (*Newsweek*, Dec. 8, 1975).

About 10 months after the much-debated 1975 *Newsweek* hit the stands, R. R. Allen, University of Wisconsin professor, delivered a speech to the Texas Speech Communication Association, which began with these words: "On the cover of *Newsweek*,

December 8, 1975, there appeared a picture of a handsome young teenager.

"His clean, well-trimmed hair, clear complexion, manicured nails, and red V neck sweater were designed to win the

"The average individual uses only about one tenth of his brain. . . . The ablest thinkers, all except geniuses, such as Leonardo da Vinci and Michelangelo were, might use a tenth more. Anyone who could use all his brain could rule the world—but probably wouldn't want to. In the human skull is a world only one-fifth explored at the most" (Abraham Merritt, **Dwellers in the Mirage**).

easy admiration of all American parents. But hark—something is wrong. He looks perplexed, and the sheets of paper on which his pen hand rests are filled with illegible scrawls and strikeovers. . . .

" 'If your children are attending college, the chances are that when they graduate they will be unable to write ordinary, expository English with any real degree of structure and lucidity. If they are in high school and planning to attend college, the chances are less than even that they will be able to write English at the minimal college level when they get there. If they are not planning to attend college, their skills in writing English may not even qualify them for secretarial or clerical work. And if they are attending elementary school, they are almost certainly not being given the kind of required reading material, much less writing instruction, that might make it possible for them eventually to write comprehensible English' " ("Do You Really Want to Know Why Johnny Can't Write—or Read, or Speak, or Listen?" *Vital Speeches of the Day*, 1976).

Allen then delved into reasons for this sad state of affairs. Whose fault could it be? Parents'? Educators'? Again I quote from *Newsweek*: "To Marshall McLuhan, the signs were clear a decade ago: 'Literary culture is through,' he said, summing up the prospective long-term impact of television. The United States, says poet Karl Shapiro, 'is in the midst of a literary breakdown.' 'We have ceased to think with words,' observes historian Jacques Barzun. 'We have stopped teaching our children that the truth cannot be told apart from the right words' " (*Newsweek*, Dec. 8, 1975).

According to study after study after study, those who do not read widely are not likely to be able to write well either, for effective writing demands verbal role models in the brain's cinematic archives. When a student in my freshman composition class sits there with a blank piece of paper and a matching blank look on the face, I can almost guarantee that the student is from a home where the TV set is on for about the current national average (seven hours and five minutes a day). Such a student, deprived of essential quiet time, reading rarely, and able to draw only from the chaotic unstructured imagery of television, finds it almost impossible to construct a coherent sentence, much less an effective paragraph.

But even later on in life, miracles still take place. My own occurred only a couple of years ago on the campus of Columbia Union College. In one of my freshman composition classes was a young man who kept dropping fur-

> *"The danger now is something that seems new and ominous: an indifference to language, a devaluation that leaves it bloodless and zombie-like. It is as if language had ceased to be important, to be worthy of attention. Television undoubtedly has something to do with that. With its chaotic parade of images, TV makes language subordinate, merely a part of the general noise" ("Can't Anyone Here Speak English?" Time, Aug. 25, 1975).*

ther and further behind. When I dialogued with him about his problems, he told me that in his home the television set was on from the moment the first person got up to the moment the last person went to bed—thus there had never been any quiet time, any time in which to discover reading—or even himself. And here he was in college, unable to keep up with either the reading or the writing. Just before the middle of the semester, he dropped the course, with the codicil that he'd be back.

Next fall, there he was, ready to try again. He told me that first day that he was planning to get the highest A in the class. I tried to avoid laughing out loud: Sure you will! But something had indeed changed: for he *did* keep up. When I asked him what had happened to make the difference, he told me: *"Books! . . . By mid semester, you had me hooked on books. I spent the rest of the semester immersed in the Weis Paperback Library, and I read books all summer—every book I could get my hands on."*

I'll never forget that evening late in April when I phoned his room in Morrison Hall—the only time I ever remember making such a call during all my years of teaching—and informed him that he had earned the highest A in the class! I could almost hear his shout all the way to Annapolis! Later on, he became an English major.

Today, more than ever, I believe in miracles. If one will only turn off the TV, at whatever age, and start a broad program of reading, life, brain-power, and the ability to articulate orally and on paper, it all will begin to come back.

But we have known about this direct correlation between reading and writing for centuries. What is only recently being revealed in media research is sending shudders through corporate America: *Not only are nonreaders unable to write well, they are also incapable of effective abstract reasoning—unable to bridge from cause to effect.* Unable to handle mathematical reasoning and statistical analysis (hence unable to arrive at accurate conclusions based on abstractions), and unable to effectively conceptualize ideas and concepts in words, these video kids now grown up represent an ever widening performance gap between American business and our international business competition.

In the October 12, 1992, Washington *Post*, Don Oldenburg reported on a meeting of the nation's most eminent researchers, clinical psychologists, educators, policymakers, and scientists who had gathered in Washington the week before to study the impact of television on the human brain. Reflecting a convention consensus, Oldenburg posed the following rhetorical questions: "Who can ignore current estimates that the average child watches 22,000 hours of television before graduating from high school—twice the amount of time spent in classrooms? Who isn't troubled by the evidence 'from the trenches,' as one participant termed the schools, where today's students seem to suffer from an epidemic of attention-deficit disorders, diminished language skills and poor reading comprehension, where teachers report that more than ever children lack analytic powers, creativity and persistence?"

Conference moderator Jane Healy (author of *Endangered Minds: Why Children Don't Think*) is known for pulling no punches—case in point, her referring to "our uneasy relationship with a medium that we suspect of rotting our children's brains."

Healy also blames the usually acclaimed PBS program *Sesame Street* for contributing to the death of reading and for misinforming children about the nature of learning. Generally speaking, Healy believes television-viewing leaves children's growing and pliable brains "disadvantaged" for the learning tasks ahead. She is outraged that any medium possibly that harmful to our progeny has barely been investigated—and is taken so lightly by so many parents.

Quite a bit of the discussion in the conference dealt with the long-term impact of TV on the brain. Apparently, more and more media scholars are beginning to suspect that TV may actually be destroying neurologically the ability of the watcher to conceptualize. Dr. Jerome Singer (coauthor of *Television and Agression*) observed that most heavy-viewing kids "show lower information, lower reading recognition or readiness to reading, lower reading levels. . . . They tend to show lower imaginativeness and less complex language use. We consistently find heavy viewing . . . is associated with more aggressive behavior."

Dr. Byron B. Reeves, Stanford professor of communications, spoke out on another issue of growing concern: the ever larger high-resolution TV screens in homes today, declaring that as the imagery becomes ever closer to life-size, inevitably it will reduce even more the recipient's ability to differentiate between actual experience and secondhand experience. Especially is Reeves concerned about the impact of large screens on children.

"What accounts for these sad findings? . . . The quality of student writing is closely correlated to the time spent watching television. Thirty percent of the fourth-graders acknowledged watching TV six hours or more a day. They were the poorest writers" (James Kilpatrick, *"Why Children Cannot Write,"* Washington Post).

Wade F. Horn, Commissioner of Health and Human Service's Administration of Children, Youth, and Families, voiced concern that "too many of America's children are arriving at the beginning of their schooling mentally unprepared to succeed—psychologically not equipped with the basic cognitive skills required for learning."

But the crowning sound bite of the conference was Oldenburg's: *"Television's electronic transmissions and programming are blowing out the brains of the remote control generation"* (Don Oldenburg, "Boob Tube Brain Drain: Probing TV's Influence on Young Minds," Washington *Post,* October 12, 1992).

Reading and writing, like most other skills, must be continually practiced in order to remain effective. If your child grows up in an environment that is not rich in newspapers, magazines, and books, chances are excellent that his or her reading and writing skills will be deficient.

Every once in a while a study comes along that sends shudders through society's thought-leaders. Such is Jane Healy's already mentioned book *Endangered Minds: Why Our Children Don't Think* (Simon & Schuster, New York, 1992). Frederick Case, of the Seattle *Times,* reviewing the study, began his review with this jolting line: "Is TV reversing the evolution of the human brain? At least one educational psychologist thinks so, and there is some evidence that supports her disturbing warnings."

> **Four Arguments for the Elimination of Television**
> *"1. TV affects the body by projecting up to 25,000 volts of artificial light into the eyes.*
> *"2. It dims the imagination by burning indelible TV images into the memory. [We have already discussed how these images are retained for life.]*
> *"3. It limits real-life experiences by keeping people in their living rooms instead of interacting with neighbors, friends, family, and each other.*
> *"4. It is biased toward the coarse, the bold, and the obvious . . . and hate over love, death over life, violence over harmony"* (Jerry Mander, *"Four Arguments for the Elimination of Television,"* Mother Earth News, Sept.-Oct., 1978).

Healy had been rocked by a landmark Canadian study dealing with people of all ages living in a small British Columbia town near Banff—it measured their creativity just before TV was introduced and then again two years later. The findings? *Both children and adults suffered a 20 percent decrease in creativity!*

According to the study's coordinator, psychology professor Tannis MacBeth Williams, in addition to the dramatic decrease in creativity, the researchers discovered "reduced persistence at problem solving, greater sex-role stereotyping, and a dramatic increase in verbal and physical aggressive behavior in both sexes."

Healy went on to note that "one of the most serious charges leveled against TV-viewing is that it robs children of the chance to develop their own mental pictures—the kind of visual imagery that helps in solving math and science problems. . . . A solution advocated by Yale University researcher Jerome Singer is to withhold TV completely until a child's reading and learning habits are well established."

Particularly disturbing, in this respect, to Healy, are the findings of Russian neuropsychologist Alexander Nuria "that learning language 'and inner speech' feeds the development of the brain's frontal area. The back of the brain is the library; the front part is the planning and executive department." In this respect, Healy called attention to the fact that today's children are so constantly being stimulated by external sources "that they have little time to reflect and talk to themselves inside their heads." In fact, Healy submitted that the growing number of learning-disabled people quite likely is a direct result of heavy TV-viewing (Frederick Case, "Minds at Risk: Is TV Detrimental to the Human Brain?" Washington *Post,* July 29, 1991).

Not long ago one of the most tragic essays I have ever read was turned in by one of my freshman students. He admitted that he had developed very poor study habits at home, where the TV was rarely off. Unable to write well, unable to read and comprehend complex material, unable even to communicate well with his peers, he felt that his life was already a dead-end street.

You see, television viewing is passive, not active. At least with print and radio, the mind translates abstract words into its own visual imagery. Whereas, as McLuhan warned us, TV fires imagery full-blown into the brains of those watching. And the more that these prefab images becloud your child's brain, the less likely your child is ever to think creatively about anything.

How could one be creative if he or she no longer thought original thoughts or arrived at conclusions on his or her own?

A specialist in child creativity recently observed that your preschool child, when offered the option of playing in a sandpile or watching *Masterpiece Theatre* on TV, ought to stay in the sandpile, for the lessons and skills being acquired contribute to adult creativity, whereas the other experience, as fine as it may be, nevertheless remains a passive one.

One of the most provocative books of our time is the famed Princeton scholar Alvin Kernan's book *The Death of Literature*. Asked to synthesize his thesis for the Washington *Post*, Kernan did so: "Literature: R.I.P."

As we come to the end of what Kernan calls the "Gutenberg Era," ominous signs appear on the horizon, such as one after another of the top library science schools of the nation closing in recent years—includ-

> *"The past is gone, and so is the old literature with its authors of imaginative genius and crystalline works of perfect art and unchanging truth, the great march of words down the centuries—Homer, Shakespeare, Balzac. But if literature is to survive in some diminished form, positive ways to speak of it must be found again"* *(Alvin Kernan, "Literature: R.I.P." Washington Post, Nov. 18, 1990).*

ing the flagship Columbia University's School of Library Science.

It may not be, perhaps, too farfetched to conjecture that print might yet be brought off the endangered species list *if* enough parents and thought-leaders wake up in time to the realization that mastery of reading, writing, and abstract reasoning skills are far more important than is the mere ability to receive celluloid visual imagery.

CHAPTER 6

Squandering God's Greatest Gift: Time

Gene was one of my closest and dearest friends . . . in those days gone by. No one loved word games more than he. On Saturday nights we'd haul the kids over to the home of whoever was host for the evening and start in on word games. Our favorite was hinky-pinky, a game in which everyone tried to guess the sound-alike words the lead player had in mind. I'll never forget one night when Gene had us all stumped. It was one of those really tough ones—a four-syllable thing. Well, we finally gave up . . . but in the wee hours one of us thought of it. Being younger then, wacky, and confirmed nightowls, we woke the other players up and decided finding the answer was reason enough to get up and go on over and wake up poor Gene and Grace. So we got our clothes on and banged on his door until, groggy-eyed, he finally stumbled to the door—only to be enthusiastically greeted by his loony colleagues. Always a good sport, he invited us in . . . and we gleefully shouted out, "Knickerbocker liquorlocker!" It was very late before any of us got back to sleep.

Well, the years passed, and Gene became academic dean of the college. The games and scintillating conversations, the book discussions, the concerts and films we would attend together, the potlucks and eating out—the whole planet was fair game to those of us who were fortunate enough to be part of Gene's circle of friends.

Then, on one never-to-be-forgotten day, the campus and community were thunderstruck to hear that Dr. Gene Thomsen had cancer—incurable, terminal bone cancer. And he in the prime of his life! There seemed no valid reason for such a thing. Here he was at the peak of his career, with so much creativity still unused.

We dreaded seeing him . . . but knowing Gene, we shouldn't have. He was as cheerful as always, with his sense of humor absolutely unimpaired. If it was the good Lord's will that he go, then he'd just enjoy to the fullest each day that was left.

He always had . . . but now he savored each moment even more, if that were possible. Gradually he began to slow down. Gene insisted on going to work for as long as it was humanly possible to do so. My office window was where I could see him get out of his car and eke his way across to the administration building. Initially he'd make it across in a few minutes. Then it slowed to 5, to 10, to 15, to a half hour, to an hour—and still he inched his way across.

Finally he was taken to the hospi-

"*Look to this day!*
For it is life, the very life of life.
In its brief course
Lie all the verities and realities of your
existence:
The bliss of growth
The glory of action
The splendor of achievement,
For yesterday is already a dream
And tomorrow is only a vision,
But today well lived
Makes every yesterday a dream of
happiness
And every tomorrow a vision of hope.
Look well, therefore, to this day!
Such is the salutation to the dawn"
(Kalidasa).

tal. After being there for a while, he summoned his doctors, looked at them with that clear-eyed gaze he had, and said, "Don't try to fool me . . . How much time do I have?" He was answered as candidly as the doctors knew how. Then Gene said, "Please have me taken back to Keene—I want to die at home."

He was. And those last days were breath-by-breath agony to him, for his body was collapsing in upon itself. His face got darker and more emaciated-looking. And still he laughed, and still he joked. We saved our fears for outside the door. And finally, mercifully, he was gone. Grace phoned me, asking a favor. When I inquired what it was, she responded that Gene had always lived his life with a poem as his day-to-day motivation. That poem was the reason he lived every hour, every minute, every second to the fullest extent of its tether. She had never thought to ask him where it came from or who wrote it, but she did remember that it had originated in India, and a key line was "Salutation to the Dawn." Could I find it in time to have it printed on the cover of the funeral program?

After ransacking several libraries, I found it was Kalidasa's "Salutation to the Dawn." I discovered that Kalidasa is recognized as perhaps the most illustrious writer of ancient Sanskrit, having lived, perhaps, in the third century A.D. and written such master-pieces as *Sakuntala* and *Vikramorvasi*. Sadly, we in the West know little of him—mainly, just this brief poem. But there are far worse things to be remembered for than these powerful lines—recalled for more than a millennium and a half.

Since that time I too have lived close to these words . . . and shared them with others as often as I could. In brief, Kalidasa's message is that if we would live a life worth living, then we must remember one great truth: Each day is a miniature lifetime, with a beginning, a middle, and an end; each daily segment of our lives has the potential to be enriched by "the bliss of growth," "the glory of action," "the splendor of achievement."

And Kalidasa reminds us of these great truths as well:

"For yesterday is already a dream
And tomorrow is only a vision,"

which leaves us, of course: *today*. Well lived, today bestows upon us that priceless legacy:

"Every yesterday" a "dream of happiness";
"Every tomorrow" a "vision of hope."
"Look well, therefore, to this day!"

> *I dedicate this section to Gene Thomsen. Each person who uses this poem as a motivation for making life a success will help make Dr. Thomsen's life and influence live on.*

Again and again in His life, ministry, parables, and sayings, Christ hammered home lessons dealing with time management. He urged that we develop to the utmost every talent God has lent us during our brief tenure on this planet. Richard Fredericks, Professor of Religion at Columbia Union College, in studying this aspect of Christ's ministry, pointed out to me that the entire New Testament is evidently intended to rouse people out of apathy into active service for others. And we have already noted that TV is the greatest apathy-producing device ever invented.

One of my favorite authors, Ellen G. White, in her book *Christ's Object Lessons*, discusses at length the subject of time. She writes: "Our time belongs to God. Every moment is His, and we are under the most solemn obligation to improve it to His glory. *Of no talent He has given will He require a more strict account than of our time*" (p. 342; italics supplied).

Clearly, then, if there is any aspect of our lives that God is going to expect a detailed accounting of, it will have to do with how we spent the bullion of the universe—time. Most of us waste a great deal of it, even without the television variable.

But with TV it is mighty difficult to see how many of our lives can be validly defended, for it is the greatest time-annihilator ever invented.

"The value of time is beyond computation. Christ regarded every moment as precious, and it is thus that we should regard it. Life is too short to be trifled away" (Ellen G. White, Christ's Object Lessons, p. 342).

Even if God did not hold us strictly accountable, it would seem only natural that we would want our lives to represent a real difference in the world—somehow, somewhere, we all desire to be remembered. None of us wish merely to have been born; to have breathed, eaten, drunk, slept, grown; to have studied, earned a living, married, had children, raised them, worked until retirement, lived a little longer—and died. No, all of us—even criminals—want our names to mean something. We want somebody to care when we go and after we are gone.

Before TV, people *did* take time out to make a difference in each other's lives, to grow continually in knowledge and skills, to enjoy the simple things of life: the dawn, the birds, the love light on a face, the unexpected hug, the opportunity to take a walk with a child, to listen to a new piece of music, to read a book, to make a new friend, to explore a new road or trail, to write a letter, to sew a quilt, to help a neighbor, to help out community or assist in church, to take time to notice a rainbow or flower.

Now let's look at some current statistics:

1. It is said that many preschoolers spend two thirds of all their waking hours in front of the TV set. It has been documented that the average preschooler will have spent over 5,000 hours watching television before entering first grade. That is much more than the class time it takes to earn a four-year college degree!

2. The average high school graduate will have spent some 22,000 hours in front of the TV set (9,000 more hours than he or she has spent in a classroom).

3. According to the latest figures (the number has been steadily climbing for a half century), the average American watches TV a little more than 30 hours a week.

But, bad as that is, it reveals only part of the story: Veronis, Suhler & Associates (a reputable investment banking house in New York, which specializes in the communications industry), in the fall of 1992 published some figures that ought to concern us all.

Of the 8,760 hours in a year,

- sleep consumes (at 7½ hours a night) 2,737 hours
- full-time work consumes 1,824 hours

Larger by far than either sleep or work are the hours claimed by the media—more than 9 hours a day!

- TV (including cable)—4 hours and 9 minutes a day
- Radio (on job, driving, at home)—3 hours
- Recorded music—36 minutes
- Daily newspaper—28 minutes
- consumer book—16 minutes
- consumer magazines—14 minutes
- home videos—7 minutes
- movies in theaters—2 minutes

As is painfully obvious, we allocate about eight times as much time to nonprint media as we do to print! Not too many years ago it was not so: We were known around the world as the greatest nation on earth—and our emphasis on the learning process was a prime reason for that success. Today, we have plummeted to a lowly 24th position in per capita reading of books. In 1991 we spent $108 billion on the media itself, with advertisers paying an additional $80 billion to bring it to us, making it the ninth largest business in America (Richard Harwood, "PBS vs MTV: So Many Media, So Little Time," Washington *Post*, Sept. 2, 1992).

Is it any wonder that our civilization is crumbling from within and that we have lost our competitive edge to other nations? If ever a national Esau sold its soul for a mess of pottage—it is we.

◆ ◆ ◆

Great people have one uniform character trait: they value the seconds, the minutes of life—not regarding any sliver of time as valueless.

If we want our lives to have been worth living—we can do no less, for

> "The clock of life is wound but once,
> And no man has the power
> To tell just when the hand will stop
> On what day—or what hour.
> Now is the only time you have,
> So live it with a will.
> Don't wait until tomorrow—
> The hands may then be still"
> *(Author Unknown)*.

As we learned from Kalidasa's "Salutation to the Dawn," there are three divisions of time: yesterday, today, and tomorrow. Many of us waste our lives because we are either living in the past or trying to anticipate the future. *Yesterday* is gone, never to return. Not all the gold in Fort Knox can buy back a second of it; hence time spent on regret is futile. *Tomorrow* is not a certainty—indeed, it may never come. Fortunately for us, the Lord has not seen fit to endow us with knowledge of future events. But He guarantees us strength only for *today*. Consequently, we should dedicate every ounce of energy we possess to the one segment of time we can do anything about—*this day*.

CHAPTER 7

The Killing Fields of Substance Abuse

An amazing 74 percent of all pre-65 deaths are preventable. They are the result of either lifestyle or environment— probably, in most cases, the two go together.

Substance abuse has been with us throughout history, but it is doubtful if ever a society has destroyed itself with such systematic thoroughness, in this respect, as ours is doing today. Undoubtedly substance abuse goes hand in hand with forsaking God and Christ-centered values. For Christians who believe—as Scripture declares—that the body is the temple through which the human interacts with the divine, it would be unthinkable to destroy that crucial conduit.

Furthermore, without a belief in God and in the hereafter, there comes a feeling that there is no tomorrow beyond this life. If, then, this life appears devoid of positive values, of reasons to live, why not terminate life sooner rather than later? This, substance abuse does— some of it just takes longer than others to do the job.

The cost to society is so high that it

> "... medical bills for smoking-related illnesses account for an estimated $50 billion a year. . . . Medical authorities attribute some 600,000 deaths a year directly to tobacco use. It's what motivates anti-tobacco activists in their nationwide fight to tighten restrictions on public smoking and cigarette advertising" (Don Oldenburg, "Tobacco's Last Gasp?" Washington Post, Feb. 23, 1993).

is quite possible that the attendant health costs alone will bankrupt our nation. As more and more people have their minds and souls short-circuited by substance abuse, fewer and fewer productive citizens will remain to pay the bills. Each drug-induced dropout makes it that much tougher for the rest of us. So it is not true, as so many addicts maintain, that in destroying themselves, they hurt no one else!

First, there is *tobacco*. We are informed by the U.S. surgeon general that more than 400,000 Americans die each year from tobacco-related causes—these represent only those cases they can prove! The actual figure is considerably higher.

To get this in true perspective, let's note the following

"A study undertaken by the Center for Disease Control found that the cause of death of those under the age of 65 could be subdivided as follows: 53 percent—due to lifestyle; 21 percent—due to environment; 9 percent—due to the health-care system; 17 percent—due to human biology" (undated bulletin from the U. S. Human Resources Department).

statistics: 58,000 American soldiers died in the Vietnam War; 55,000, in the Korean War; 417,000, in World War II; and 127,000, in World War I. Altogether they total up to roughly the equivalent of *one year's worth of tobacco-related deaths* in this country alone! And, unbelievably, we continue to subsidize the growing of tobacco, and worse yet, to permit tobacco companies to advertise. The tobacco-related health costs that the rest of us pay for is staggering.

Ellen Goodman, in a recent Washington *Post* column, commented on Surgeon General Antonia Novella's (and leaders of the American Medical Association) outrage at R. J. Reynolds' fiendishly clever Joe Camel tobacco advertising campaign: it resulted in an incredible leap from 0.5 to 32.8 percent of Camel's share of the illegal children's cigarette market.

Since so many adult American smokers continue to quit smoking, tobacco companies criminally target underage children and youth. Ninety percent of smokers are thus addicted during their first 20 years—and then they are hooked!

Next, there are *alcoholic beverages.* Who knows how many die from liquor-related causes each year? We *do know* that most of

Every day, on the way to work, I pass an elementary school. Next door, right on the edge of the sidewalk, are two large impossible-to-miss Joe Camel signs. Such an act borders on the criminal!

our highway fatalities are direct results—a good share of them innocent victims. We *do know* that liquor has, over and over, proved to be a stepping-stone to hard drugs. We *do know* that we thereby lose millions of days of productivity in our work force every year. We *do know* that liquor is perhaps the major contributing cause to our epidemic levels of child battering, spouse battering, and violence. We *do know* that it is inextricably woven into our crime statistics everywhere we look.

As early as 1976, Ernest Noble, director of the National Institute of Alcohol Abuse, declared that TV was directly responsible for the doubling of young drinkers in the previous 20 years. He strongly condemned the media for its portrayal, in both programming and advertising, of people as successful and more sexually desirable because of drinking. And as for sports and Olympic alcohol-related advertising, he solemnly warned: "Children are bound to want to imitate such figures" ("Drinkers Double; TV Blamed," Fort Worth *Star-Telegram*, Sept. 24, 1976).

In 1988 we were informed by the Associated Press that children can now name more booze brands than they can presidents—and television is the reason. The significance of this sad state of affairs can hardly be overemphasized. Thanks to the media, the average child will now have seen more than 75,000 alcoholic beverages consumed before he or she reaches drinking age!

In the mid-1970s the *Christian Science Monitor* conducted a survey on liquor ads on television. The findings: "In a recent survey . . . [it was noted] that there

> *"In a country where children of 12 can routinely name at least five alcoholic beverages but not five presidents, it's time to turn off the television and think about where we are going" (Jack Anderson and Dale Van Atta, "Fighting the Dumbness Trend," Washington Post, 1990).*

were scenes involving hard liquor *ten times more than soft drinks* were used." Yet in real life, soft drinks are consumed *16 times more than liquor!* (See "Tele-Addiction: A Habit That's Hard to Kick," *These Times*, Apr. 1978.)

As we can plainly see, the media's gross distortion of the average incidence of liquor consumption in this country is dramatically weighted in the wrong direction. Thanks to this media barrage, no matter what parents tell the child about the effects of alcoholism, the sheer number of liquor ads is likely to outweigh all the previous parental instruction.

And finally, there are *drugs*—all kinds of them—eating away at the very heart of our nation. We now worry about whether or not our car-pool driver, our bus driver, our train engineer, our airline pilot, has been on drugs. Is the surgeon who operates on Mother high? We worry on so many, many levels.

But most of all, knowing how the drug habit destroys an individual's moral control center, we worry about what it is doing to our children, our relatives, our friends, and about what our odds are likely to be if we meet one of these addicts on a downer as he or she is seeking for money for another fix. We have no security anymore.

And the media—especially television—is directly responsible for much of this hell we daily endure, this hell that we continue to permit by our passivity—our inexcusable tendency to do nothing.

The media record in all these substance abuse areas adds up to a national tragedy!

Directors of the Washington-based Council on Children, Media, and Advertising ascribe no small part of the blame for hard drug use to the 1,000-plus over-the-counter drug ads that children are exposed to each year—ads which condition them to accept drugs as a normal part of their lives. The step to hard drugs is but a short one from there.

In stark contrast—which makes one wonder if in some respects we are losing rather than gaining ground—according to the ancient Babylonian Code of Hammurabi, it was punishable by death to pander advertising to a child!

CHAPTER 8

♦

Sexuality and the Occult

God created us with a strong sex drive, so the drive itself is not evil. But we have perverted that drive, twisted it, destroyed all the beauty of it—demoting sex from a God-given source of joy and long-term love and commitment to a mere mechanical act, carrying with it not even the saving grace of friendship. In this respect, our society is no better than ancient societies with their temple prostitutes.

For millenniums one factor that tended to contribute to virginity was the strong likelihood that sexual intercourse would result in pregnancy. Unwed mothers being ostracized with society's red letter meant that fear rather than inclination kept many in earlier times from straying too far. But the Pill, other birth-control devices, and the easy access to abortions has totally changed the world we live in. These factors have given women considerably more power over their heterosexual relationships than was possible when the average American husband openly boasted about how he kept his wife subservient by keeping her "barefoot and pregnant."

Now, reversing history, more and more often it is the woman who is the aggressor, the one who initiates or terminates relationships. Nevertheless, the media still tend to demean women. They still tend to project her as more of a sex object than a thinking, caring being. She is still locked into this historical stereotype, and there continue to be women who will sell themselves, prostitute their better selves, in exchange for lucrative contracts and comparatively large sums of money.

Almost nothing in the media encourages young girls to grow up virgins and to bring that virginity as their greatest gift to their chosen mate. Neither is there encouragement for a boy to save his first sexual experience for the woman he wishes to share the rest of

> *"Teenagers see an estimated 14,000 sexual references and innuendos a year on television, and only 150 of those deal with sexual responsibility, abstinence, or contraception. Therefore, the many implicit and explicit messages on television that promote alcohol consumption or unprotected sexual activity are a cause for concern" (American Academy of Pediatrics, April 1990).*

his life with. Rather, the opposite is true: They are barraged with the message that sexuality is all in all, that if you will just find the right sexual chemistry, you will achieve real fulfillment. Then the media spike their own cannons by depicting the emptiness that inevitably follows sex without commitment, love without undergirding friendship—even to the exclusion of liking!

There could be no possible better place than here to inject the conditioning element of the media into our discussion. Richard Fredericks has spent considerable time delving into the methodology psychologists use in order to change behavior patterns in their patients. He did this because he wanted to compare their approaches with media methodology. What he discovered rocked him on his heels.

Standard in the profession is a six-step procedure that has proved to be virtually failure-proof in changing behavior:

1. The person views familiar images in a comfortable, nonthreatening situation. He or she is completely relaxed. No emotional arousal is noted.

2. Certain images or scenes known to arouse emotional reactions are introduced. Relaxation ceases.

"We are like peasants living in a battle zone. There is death all around us. We are hardened to it. We do not even ignore it; we make it now our staple entertainment. . . . We think the Romans were brutes because they staged death games in the arena. Now we simulate them for children on television and in the films. . . . Millions of people line up to see a child masturbate herself with a crucifix" (Morris West, "We Are Like Peasants," Harlequin).

3. The scene shifts, or viewing is interrupted. Viewer's arousal is not allowed time to react.

4. Viewer is given a respite period of approximately one minute, during which he or she resumes a relaxed mental and physical stage. This is facilitated by eating or drinking.

5. As the viewer's emotions subside, viewing of nonthreatening images has resumed. Subject is completely relaxed. No strong feelings are noted.

6. The cycle is repeated.

Notice how perfectly this six-step process mirrors the rhythm of television—even to the commercial, tailor-made for item 4.

Fredericks notes that in order for the desensitizing to work effectively, there needs to be a number of con- stants:

"This technique is effective in stripping people of their feelings by whittling away at emotions until a person can remain relaxed, undisturbed and unmoved even as he watches scenes that had originally occa- sioned his gravest concern, acutest distress, most painful anxiety" (Richard Fredericks, "Television and the Christian Family," IV:10).

1. There must be a pleasant atmo- sphere that is famil- iar, secure, and un- threatening to the patient.

2. The contents and arrangements must be consistent and predictable, allowing complete relaxation. Thus, for maximum results, the ideal lab would be the subject's own living room.

3. All intense emotions must be discouraged for any extended duration.

4. Presenting themes or concepts in the context of drama assists significantly in the acceptance of the process.

5. Social reinforcement (viewing the scenes with a respected or loved person) assists in acceptance. The ideal, of course, would be a family sitting together.

As to the objectives, procedures, and likely results, Fredericks lists the following. For this process, psychologists use fantasy materials that are specifically designed to "trigger new thought patterns in the imagination to extinguish emotional reactions to ideas or events a patient formerly feared or rejected. Strong feelings against something are eliminated and replaced with casual accep- tance. The responses change because the process has altered values and attitudes—*what we once ran from we can now abide with*" ("Television and the Christian Family," IV:10).

"Those who practice this technique claim that *the emotionless state it brings about becomes generalized* so that when a person trained in imaginal desensitization comes upon *scenes in real life that are the same or similar to those he has seen over and over again in imaginary dramas he can even then remain detached and unmoved by them*" (ibid.).

As to how long it takes to get the job done, Fredericks notes that "therapists who use systematic desensitization claim that it usually only requires 20 to 30 exposure/sessions to alter a person's feelings from acceptance to rejection, or rejection to acceptance" (*ibid.*).

So now let's apply this conditioning process to the amoral values so vividly portrayed by the media: 20 to 30 exposures, at current rates of watching, would have been achieved within 7 to 14 days! Everything after that is but a nailing on of the lid to the character and behavioral changes!

Now, remember we are not even talking about children here—the job could be done much more quickly with them. We are talking about adults! You and me.

Furthermore, almost nothing in the media encourages those who are already married to remain so. Rather, every possible reason and inducement to do otherwise is introduced again, again, and again, gradually reducing to rubble even stronger defense systems.

Pat Robertson articulated the problem in a June 1987 *Sunshine*: "Instead of absolutes, our youth have been given situation ethics. . . . Instead of a clear knowledge of right and wrong, they have been told 'if it feels good, do it.' Instead of self-restraint they are often taught self-gratification and hedonism."

When such powerful counterbalances are removed, the effects on society are cataclysmic. Case in point: A recent television special dealt with a fast-rising social problem—an epidemic of *children raping other children*!

"We must face evil, not run from it; because when we run, evil pursues. Evil must be 'stared down.' Thousands are neurotics today because they try to escape problems, only to face bigger ones down the line. This is something we need to teach our children early. Many children start such neuroses by lying to avoid unpleasant issues, and the habit becomes a malignant one" (Dale Evans Rogers).

Along with sexuality—even intertwined with it—is more and more of the mystic, of the occult. Increasingly, depictions of the occult are so vividly and persuasively portrayed—and portrayed so repeatedly—that even the person who has been raised a Christian will begin to experience blurred focus, will begin to believe in the occult subconsciously while still consciously professing otherwise. It seems clear that the only safety for the Christian is not to watch such insidious portrayals at all.

Tony Muha, an Annapolis clinical psychologist, urges parents to set limits on what influences their children: "The words of some of today's biggest rock stars promote a variety of messages that often shock parents when they actually pay attention to the lyrics. Some common themes in the music many kids are singing to themselves include sexual promiscuity, violence against women, racial and religious slurs, satanic worship, drug use, and suicide. . . . In the same way a child learns his ABCs from listening and repeating what he hears, the process of memorizing the messages contained in music will provide powerful influences in a child's mind. . . . Parents would never allow food that they knew was poisoned to be taken into their children's bodies. Unfortunately, we don't often ask ourselves if what we are allowing to go into a child's mind contains a poisonous point of view" ("Set Limits on What Influences Your Child," *The Capital*, Jan. 10, 1991).

As for television fare, Muha notes: "Children assume the values that are being portrayed in the programs are correct because the people they see in these programs seem glamorous and happy. But 80 percent of the sexual scenes are between unmarried people, and in fewer than 1 percent of the scenes is there any reference to birth control made. The message to the child is that sex outside of marriage is the norm and birth control is not often practiced. Frequently sex and violence are associated with each other. Are these the values you want your child to acquire?" (*ibid.*).

Film critic Michael Medved (co-host of *Sneak Previews* on PBS) has been much in the news lately himself. The reason is his new book, *Hollywood vs. America: The War on Traditional Values*. In an article for the Washington *Post*, Medved summed up some of his major contentions.

For one, he ridicules the media for taking credit for some things (positive plugs for condoms, registering to vote, assigning designated drivers when drinking takes place, helping to save rain forests, etc.) but paradoxically insisting that the "violence, hedonism, and selfishness so often featured in their work will have no real world consequences whatever. . . .

"Hollywood apologists implausibly insist that Murphy Brown or other fictional characters in TV shows exert no influence whatever on their fans, thereby ignoring the fact that millions of young people imitate pop-culture icons, dressing like Madonna or Michael Jackson, swaggering like the Terminator or repeating the rude quips of Bart Simpson. . . . Isn't it absurd that a business that charges hundreds of thousands of dollars for a few minutes of commercial airtime in the belief that fleeting images can sell anything from canned goods to candidates, then turns around and asserts that the hours of programming that surround those brief advertisements have no impact on the audience?"

Medved goes on to develop his thesis that Hollywood appears to be deliberately attempting to destroy the traditional family, noting that film idols such as "Goldie Hawn and Kurt Russell, Woody Allen and Mia Farrow, Susan Sarandon and Tim Robbins, Jessica Lange and Sam Sheppard, Sean Penn and Robin Wright, Farrah Faucett and Ryan O'Neal, Jack Nicholson and Rebecca Broussard, Eddie Murphy, Glenn Close, Christopher Reeve, Mick Jagger, Al Pacino, Rod Stewart, Ed Asner, William Hurt, Sting, Ice Cube and many others all seem to make a point of avoiding or delaying marriage, even after they bring children into the world."

> *"There was once a time when Hollywood was a shining beacon on the public scene. Actors and performers were our heroes, and as children we looked up to them wanting to emulate their deeds and their values. Today's entertainers are still our children's heroes. Some heroes!"* (L. Brent Bozell III, *"Peddlers of Smut,"* Washington Post, Feb. 23, 1993).

Medved noted that, in earlier times, Hollywood at least paid lip service to traditional family values. Not anymore! "Contemporary entertainers win the admiration of their peers and the Hollywood press for challenging, rather than respecting, the old-fashioned family pieties."

Even in child-centered films such as *Baby Boom, Three Men and a Baby,* and *Look Who's Talking,* Medved observes that, in each case, the underlying message of the film was crystal clear: "Babies may be rewarding and irresistible, but they are best enjoyed without the inconvenient entanglements of marriage."

TV's record in this respect, submits Medved, conveys even more blatantly anti-traditional values. Everywhere the norm is single-parenthood. In the 1991 season alone, of the seven pregnancies featured

"Since the 1989 Webster decision, numerous TV series and TV movies have dedicated themselves to the abortion question. All have supported a woman's right to an abortion. Not one has ever championed the right to life of a child. To say that the marketplace determines the product is to say that there is no such thing as a right-to-life movement" (L. Brent Bozell III, "Peddlers of Smut," Washington Post, Feb. 23, 1993).

during prime time—only one mother was married. *Time* magazine writers ruefully observed in November 1991 that "traditional child-bearing has virtually disappeared from the airwaves" (Michael Medved, "Hollywood Chic: Illegitimacy and Hypocrisy—Family Values Suffer at the Hands of Pop Idols," Washington *Post,* Oct. 4, 1992).

CHAPTER 9
◆

Three Bad Checks:
Advertising, News,
and Language

Yes, three bad checks. Three accounts that are—even by congressional standards—heavily overdrawn.

The Awesome Power of Advertising

The advertisements your children see not only contribute in a major way to greed, but also are full of lifestyle statements that are totally antithetical to Christian values. In fact, by themselves they represent a vast body of misinformation far more powerful than church, schools, and home combined. Twenty-five percent of children's programming is commercials, and children see more than 1,000 drug (cough, colds, etc.) ads a year.

One of the most powerful critics in early media research was Jerry Mander. In "Four Arguments for the Elimination of Television," he detailed an epiphany that changed the course of his life. During a cruise down the Dalmatian coast, as he leaned against the deck rail and observed some of the most magnificent scenery the world has to offer, it suddenly struck him that there was a "film" between himself and the unrolling panorama. It was as if the experience stopped short of his eyes, and what made it through was devoid of any intensity or deep feeling! Something dramatically wrong was happening, but it had not been so when as a child he had intensely reveled in nature.

"It wasn't that nature was boring. It was that nature had become irrelevant to me, absent from my life. Through mere lack of exposure and practice, I'd lost the ability to feel it, tune into it, or care about it. Life moved too fast for that now" (*Mother Earth News*, Sept.-Oct. 1978).

And advertising was one of the key reasons this was so. Early in his career Mander had enjoyed a business partnership with that advertising genius, the late Howard Gossage. "Gossage knew that there was more to the problem of advertising work than the way it emphasizes trivia. He would rage about the function itself, speak-

THE FAMILY CIRCUS BIL KEANE

*"I'm only seven years old and already
tired of commercials."*

ing of it as an invasion of privacy on an order far more extreme than the merely rude telephone solicitation, the door-to-door salesperson, or even the computer file on your credit. *It was an invasion of the mind which altered behavior, altered people"* (*ibid.*; italics supplied).

The commercials tell your children that it is the *products* that will determine their identity, not what is inside. Neil Postman, in a *U.S. News & World Report* interview, observed that in the first 20 years of our lives, we will have seen about a million commercials. "This makes the TV commercial the most voluminous information source in the education of youth. . . . A commercial teaches a child three interesting things. The first is that all problems are resolvable. The second is that all problems are resolvable fast. And the third is that all problems are resolvable fast through the agency of some technology (drug, detergent, car, computer)" (Jan. 19, 1981).

And what are the other messages preached by these ever-so-convincing commercials?

1. *Products—not character—determine your identity.* Dr. Kenneth Curtis of Gateway Films labels this an "insidious assault on the Christian view, holding that life consists of things possessed, the opposite of Jesus' teaching" (cited in George Cornell, "Commercials," Fort Worth *Star-Telegram*, Mar. 12, 1977).

Philip Whidden put it this way: "The main destructive force in advertising is one that teaches us that we are not good enough as we have been made in Christ's creation

> *"As the kids grow older their attitudes toward commercials move from innocent acceptance to outrage about these ads that mislead, and finally to a cynical recognition of what they perceive as adult hypocrisy. According to a study by Columbia University psychology professor Thomas Bever, TV ads may be 'permanently distorting children's views of morality, society, and business'"* ("What TV Does to Kids," Newsweek, Feb. 21, 1977).

and His re-creation. *We are never good enough in Madison Avenue's eyes.* If we bathed, swathed, doused, plucked, shaved, dyed, bleached, rinsed, imbibed, smoked, shopped, and deodorized as our full-time occupation, we could never keep up with the ad man's idea of what a worthy human is. . . . [Advertisers] have blatantly anti-Christian ideas about what is worthwhile" ("Seeing Through a Crass, Starkly Cunning Business," *Insight*, Mar. 8, 1977).

2. *"All problems are resolvable, all problems are resolvable fast, all problems are resolvable through some agency of technology"*—thus there is no need for a God.

3. *Junk food and over-the-counter drugs are better than a healthful diet.*

4. *Loudness, crudeness, uncouthness, ungraciousness, obnoxiousness, rudeness are all highly desirable qualities to live by.*

5. *Children and youth know far more about life than parents,*

teachers, ministers, and other adults.

    6. *Liquor and substance abuse of all kinds is cool.*

    Longtime TV critic Tom Shales observed, "Much of the behavior by characters in commercials that is supposed to look adorable borders on the reprehensible. In beer ads, men are told it's the coolest thing in the world to sit around all day sloshing brew with the guys. And yet, wonder of wonders, none of these lushes ever seems to get the slightest bit tipsy, much less a genuine snootfull. Somebody's wife ought to show up in one of these commercials and take somebody home. Dragging him by the ears if necessary" ("Tube Flunks Again as an Ethics Teacher," Fort Worth *Star-Telegram*, Dec. 29, 1980).

    7. *Sexuality is far more important than true caring and commitment.*

    8. *Lusting for what does not belong to us is a highly desirable character trait.*

News That Is Not News

    An alarmingly high number of Americans—enough to lower newspaper readership to only 30 percent of the population—today gain their primary impressions about what is happening in the world by listening to television news. It's also frightening in terms of the future of our democracy, because an uninformed electorate is a loose cannon on deck. Our forefathers took seriously the responsibility of securing and maintaining our hard-fought

> *"The evening news runs 22 minutes, which means that if a presidential candidate gets 30 seconds of a speech on the air, he is lucky. We no longer get visions or complete thoughts. We're lucky to get complete sentences. Complexity gives way to a new kind of simplistic, hyped-up campaign charge and countercharge, mistake and seizing on mistake. Substance becomes obliterated"* (David Halberstam, "How Television Failed the American Voter," Parade, Jan. 11, 1981).

freedoms. Today, to be a reasonably informed voter, one ought to subscribe to two newspapers, a local and a large regional; a news magazine; and listen, if time, to key commentary on radio and television. Anything much short of this is inadequate for the task.

But back to television. Some years ago Erik Barnouw observed that "television newspeople depend largely on pseudoevents. They decide before anything happens what's going to be important. The only exceptions are fires and floods and other catastrophes that last long enough to get the cameras there. Everything else is an arranged event. . . . This puts an awful lot of power into the hands of people who are in a position to arrange things of that sort. . . . Fighting went on in Angola for 10 years before we suddenly had it on the evening news. Things that don't happen on the tube don't seem to have really happened. . . . What happens on TV sticks in the mind. It's brighter. It's in living color that is more living than anything in your own life. It has fantastic authority" ("A Dangerous Malaise Ahead for TV Viewers," *U.S. News & World Report*, Mar. 1, 1976).

Barnouw noted that, in a documented instance, a TV camera crew covering a Chicago riot actually tried to get bystander kids to loot in order to "imitate" reality. "TV news . . . has little to do with news. It amounts to show biz."

And when the text of the entire evening news amounts to no more than half a page of newspaper copy, we can see how little substance is possible. Not to mention the sad reality that TV news is heavily slanted to the sensational and the lurid—as well as staged-for-television activities that, as a result of being filmed and shown, become news whether they ought to be or not.

Dr. Marshall Vary, in *The Harding Journal of Religion and Psychiatry,* notes that children aged 7 or younger are likely to misinterpret news stories, personalizing cause and effect. Furthermore, he warns that many scenes presented on the news are not suitable for children to see. On the other hand, older children (ages 8-12), especially the brighter, more verbal ones, are likely to be overwhelmed by the intensity of some of the stories, some even to the nightmare stage.

I can personally testify to the validity of that last statement of Dr. Vary's. During the recent Gulf war I noted several students sitting on the floor or on armchairs in the hallways near my office. These college students were so thrown off stride by the TV news that they lost their equilibrium. They just sat there reeling in sort of a circuit-overload trance. If television news coverage can affect college-age students so dramatically, just imagine the impact on a child!

Famed journalist Daniel Schorr, in a retrospective glance over his career titled "See It Not," made a number of revealing admissions about both himself and his profession. He has never been able to rest easy about his own spotty track record—for example, his deliberately choosing to interview militants like Stokely Carmichael and Rap Brown rather than moderates because of the increased likelihood that such interviews would actually be aired on live television. Nor has he been able to forget one memorable meeting with Martin Luther King, Jr. Hoping to elicit a threatening sound-bite out of King, he noticed how morose and downcast King looked. Schorr asked why.

" 'Because of you,' he said, 'and because of your colleagues in television. You try to provoke me to threaten violence, and if I don't, you will put on those who do. And by putting them on television, you will elect them our leaders. And if there is violence, will you think of your part in bringing it about?' " (Washington Post, 1992).

Schorr also called attention to the symbiotic relationship between TV and violence, especially where hostage-taking, kidnapping, and terrorism are concerned. Coverage inflames and exaggerates the act itself, and quite possibly even increases the mortality rate as well.

The Blueing of Our Lives

Ted Koppel made a deadly judgment on the value of the television medium: *"Almost everything that is said publicly these days is recorded. . . . Almost nothing of what is said is worth remembering."* If that were the only problem tied in with TV's word usage, it wouldn't be so bad, but the sad reality is this: Each year, within recent memory, television's use of language, subject matter, taboos, swearwords, sexual words, and obscenities has deteriorated further. We have reached the point where "decency" is so far back in television history that few remember when it was even a factor in programming. Today nothing—no matter how foul, no matter how crude, no matter how obscene, no matter how sacrilegious, no matter how much it may hurt someone's reputation—seems to be off limits.

"By beholding we become changed." All of us have read this and agreed, but most of us have not taken it very seriously. My most vivid example of the maxim's validity occurred a number of years ago when I was part of a painting crew in Utah. A more foul-mouthed group of people I have never associated with. I was with them only two weeks before an accident—perhaps providential—severed the relationship. For years afterward, even though foul language was totally foreign to me, whenever I was in any kind of stress, these filthy, obscene words would leap to my mouth and beg to be used! And that was the result of only two weeks!

As much as I have resisted, I too am a part of our mass culture. It's virtually impossible not to be affected by it. Even my own fairly limited exposure to the media has made heavy inroads into my innermost thoughts, motivations, drives, and behavior. These battering rams have rammed through my innermost defenses far more than I like to admit. Fortunately for me, I have a Lord who accepts me despite my frailties and many mistakes.

Naturally, with my own experience in mind, I was deeply impressed by Carol Ann Jones's letter to the Washington *Post* editor. It is without doubt one of the most powerful statements on the effects of language used and heard that I have ever come across: "While Tom Shales has done well to confront the distressing use of unsavory language on TV, he undercut his whole argument with the amazing observation that 'language does not corrupt minds or imperil souls.' . . . I strongly disagree.

"Language is the flesh and blood of communication, not only imparting information but rich with nuances. English professors grade papers not just on content and style but upon clarity of thought and expression. . . . Imprecise language reveals incomplete thought. Language and thought are married with all the subtlety and nuances of the mind in the act of expressing itself.

"Language can 'imperil souls.' It can cut as sharply as a rapier, or strike as bluntly as a bludgeon, a crude instrument designed to elicit a reaction through shock rather than communicate anything of worth.

"Tom Shales also overlooks the crux of the controversy over off-color remarks by not addressing the underpinnings of the 'tell-it-like-it-is' school so popular these days among Hollywood dons. Such a premium is placed on reproducing 'reality' in its crudest, sleaziest, and most violent form that no one weighs the negative against the positive.

"Having our noses rubbed in it, and those of our nation's children, night after night produces little redeeming social value, unless the goal is a generation of street-mouthed, jaded, uninhibited children who have been taught to think and react in the phrases of the gutter. What thoughts are bred by such abusive uses of language?

"The ancients believed that entertainment was most satisfying when it taught as well as delighted. How unfortunate that in our modern world we seem to have lost the desire to edify while enjoying life's pleasures, preferring rather to push all the necessary buttons to elicit our most base responses" (Carol Ann Jones, [Falls Church, VA]; in Washington *Post*, Sept. 22, 1990).

And what are our scriptural guidelines in this respect? Listen to Matthew 12:34-37, with television-viewing realities in the background of your mind: "For a man's words flow out of what fills his heart. A good man gives out good—from the goodness stored in his heart; a bad man gives out evil—from his store of evil. I tell you that men will have to answer at the day of judgment for *every careless word they utter*—for it is your words that will acquit you, and your words that will condemn you" (Phillips).

In Mark 7 Christ discusses the subject of this study: What we program our minds with. Certainly were Christ speaking to us in twentieth-century America, He would suggest that we judge TV by the kind of lives it causes heavy watchers to live. "It is what comes out of a man that defiles him. For from inside, out of a man's heart, come evil thoughts, acts of fornication, of theft, murder, adultery, ruthless greed, and malice; fraud, indecency, envy, slander, arrogance, and folly; these evil things all come from inside, and they defile the man" (verses 20-23, NEB).

The apostle Paul also speaks out on the issue, most notably in Romans 12, verses 1 and 2, when he urges those in the church at Rome not to—as J. B. Phillips phrases it—"let the world around you squeeze you into its own mould." Paul might as well have been talking of the programming our children watch, when he suggests to those in the church of Ephesus to: "Live your lives in love. . . . But as for sexual immorality in all its forms, and the itch to get your hands on what belongs to other people—don't even talk about such things; they are no fit subjects for Christians to talk about. The keynote of your conversation should not be coarseness or silliness or flippancy—which are

"There is no narrowing so deadly as the narrowing of man's horizon of spiritual things. No worse evil can befall him than in his course on earth to lose sight of heaven. And it is not civilization that can prevent this, it is not civilization that can compensate for it. No widening of science, no possession of abstract truth, can indemnify for an enfeebled hold on the highest and central truths of humanity. 'What shall a man give in exchange for his soul!' " (inscription, Stanford University).

quite out of place, but a sense of all that we owe to God. . . . Don't let anyone fool you with empty words. . . . Make the best use of your time, despite all the evils of these days. . . . We are up against the unseen power that controls this dark world, and spiritual agents from the very headquarters of evil" (Eph. 5:2-6:12, Phillips).

CHAPTER 10

Media Battle Between Good and Evil—No Contest

Yes, it is no contest at all. The weaponry is so lopsided. Yet almost unbelievably, Christians have remained ingloriously inert in this battle for their souls and the souls of those dear to them. Apparently most of us live in a fool's paradise, convinced that what we fill our minds and souls with will have little or no effect on behavior! Don't Christians ever consciously analyze what they see? Don't they even question whether or not those who write and produce these programs, shows, and videos are Christian or not, share their values or not? If they did, they would sober up in record time.

KUDZU by Doug Marlette.

By permission of Doug Marlette and Creators Syndicate.

Ten years ago, when the airwaves were much cleaner than they are today, a major study was conducted by S. Robert Lichter and Stanley Rothman. They interviewed in-depth (an hour each) 240 of the nation's top journalists and broadcasters (major luminaries from such blue-ribbon entities as the New York *Times*, Washington *Post*, *Wall Street Journal*, *Time*, *Newsweek*, *U.S. News & World Report*, CBS, ABC, PBS, etc.). What they discovered, in light of what is being produced, ought to surprise us not at all.

"Ninety-five percent are White. . . . Seventy-nine percent are male. . . . Ninety-three percent are college graduates; 55 percent, postgraduates. . . . Sixty-eight percent are from the Northeast or North Central—only 3 percent from entire Pacific Coast. . . . The most striking characteristic? A secular outlook. Fifty percent have no religious affiliation at all; 86 percent seldom, if ever, attend church or synagogue—only 8 percent attend regularly. Almost 25 percent were raised in Jewish homes. The survey indicates that they are strong supporters of sexual permissiveness: 90 percent believe that abortion should be permitted, 54 percent believe that adultery is not wrong, 76 percent believe that homosexuality is not wrong (85 percent believe that homosexuals should be permitted to teach in private schools). . . . It's no wonder they oppose prayer in schools; most of the media don't even believe in prayer in church or synagogue" (cited in Phyllis Schafley, "Media Elite Influential in Telling Americans What Should Be Concerns," Cleburne, Texas, *Times-Review*, Feb. 21, 1982).

Former vice president Dan Quayle may very well be remembered more for his challenging the nation's cultural elite than for any other action during his tenure of office. He had the temerity to suggest that Murphy Brown (Candace Bergen) would do the nation a disservice by having a baby out of wedlock on a televised sitcom segment. During the storm that followed, *Newsweek* put out a special issue, and the cover copy read: "The Cultural Elite / The *Newsweek* 100 / Who They Really Are."

Jonathan Alter, lead writer of the cover article, observed that Quayle was right in his contention that a cultural elite exists: "This group exists, and its values are shaping us all."

As to the cultural elite's accomplishments, Alter minced no words: "With the help of television, that elite has expanded to produce all of America's powerful and highly exportable mass culture, including our smelliest trash."

Also noted was a recent *Newsweek* poll which revealed—certainly it must have surprised no one—that Americans believe that television is almost twice as dominant an educating force as are parents.

As to who they are, Alter pointed out that "they are better educated, richer, more liberal, more mobile, less religious and less connected to conventional standards of morality than most of the public." But Alter was not yet through. Just in case the full implications of these words had yet to sink home, he followed it up with this uppercut (and his spokesman was Howard Suber of UCLA): "There are three elite groups in this country that professionally understand that they must function amorally: Hollywood, the media and politicians. . . . Each promotes and feeds off the other."

And what are they preaching? "Clergy and businessmen are generally portrayed as bad guys." "Gays and minorities are generally portrayed as good guys." "Republicans are people to laugh at." "Obscenity is dressed up as 'free expression' and sometimes paid for by the government."

Do they believe their own message? Not according to film director John Milius: "People in Hollywood don't have a shred of honest ideology among them. Like Washington's supposedly liberal lawyers who spend their days representing polluters and tobacco companies, their work and personal attitudes rarely mix."

"Is the market calling for the barrage of gay-rights themes, on television today? And is there no market for the thoughtful opinion that homosexuality is wrong? Is the market calling for movies and television shows regularly to depict businessmen as evil and corrupt? And is there no market for the positive portrayal of the free enterprise system? Is the market demanding the eco-nonsense we so often see because there is no market for science? Or are these products Hollywood chooses to sell while keeping conservative values out of the market?" (L. Brent Bozell III, "Peddlers of Smut," Washington Post, Feb. 23, 1993).

What about their view of society? "Four of the five Best Actor nominees for this year were playing psychotic characters. That shows a great dispensation on the part of the Academy to honor people in roles that show the dark side of society. . . . They're creating a world that's worse than the world in which most of us live" (*Newsweek,* Oct. 5, 1992).

Indeed, Quayle's contentions could not be easily laughed away, even though many tried. It focused all of our attention on the very unpretty picture of what Americans have become. In fact, it did more, it resulted in Columnist Jonathan Yardley's unleashing the single most devastating critique ever written about our mass culture.

"It may well be that nothing in contemporary society is more injurious to the general well-being than the mirror-image we hold up to ourselves in the bazaar of popular culture . . . the images of mass culture—especially those of television—are not merely all-pervasive, they are also remarkably consistent in character. That we could go utterly unaffected by them is inconceivable. . . .

"They portray a society in which 'traditional values'—the nuclear family, religion, education—are either non-existent or scorned; in which sexual license is absolute while its consequences, both social and moral, are lampooned or ignored; in which 'self-fulfillment' and 'self-esteem' are valued more highly than sacrifice or discipline . . . in which violence is intense, ubiquitous, and, like sexual license, oddly devoid of lasting or injurious consequences.

"What they portray is, in a phrase, a world of entertainment. It is a fantasy land in which the basest human desires—most of them having to do with titillation in one form or another—are elevated to the heights of legitimacy, given respectability by ceaseless reiteration in everything from situation comedies to feature films to popular songs to paperback novels—not to mention the broadcast and print advertisements that, it can be argued, set the table for American culture in the 1990's.

"These images and the 'values' for which they argue are quite literally inescapable. They are the dominant images of American life in these last years of the 20th Century. . . .

"Those cues seem to be especially alluring so far as sex and voilence are concerned. The constraints that civilization has built up around these deep urges have largely been torn away by mass culture. Explicit sexual imagery—imagery that only a few decades ago would have been utterly unthinkable—is routine in everything from advertising to rap music."

Yardley also called attention to James B. Twitchell's recent book *Carnival Culture*, which picks up on a major study of recent published fiction.

"It found a 61 percent increase in so-called antisocial or pro-violence themes in fiction from 1966 to 1988, and reported: 'In the past 20 years violent books have been more intensely sadistic and gruesome than anything ever making the bestseller list in American history. Satanic and horror themes have become commonplace after having been nonexistent before the 1960's. It is clear that modern readers of popular fiction are entertaining themselves with more hate-filled, sadistic and gruesome material than any previous generation of human beings in world history. The same can be said of movies, television and music, which are far more potent than print, especially for young people who have been ill-served by American education and over-sexed by mass culture. . . . It can't be mere coincidence that random violence is increasing at the same time that such violence is mythologized in mass culture; that out-of-wedlock childbirth is increasing at the same time that unfettered sexual indulgence is celebrated in the same culture; that respect for education and self-discipline is declining at the same time that the culture places higher value on inarticulate self-expression and unlimited self-gratification" (Jonathan Yardley, May 25, 1992, Washington *Post*).

And just what are the lessons they are teaching us? The conservative way of life is, at best, a continual butt of ridicule and amusement in almost all programming. And, sadly, many televan-

FRANK & ERNEST BOB THAVES FRANK & ERNEST reprinted by permission of NEA, Inc.

I UNDERSTAND IT'S OKAY TO BREAK ONE IF YOU GO ON TV AND SAY YOU'RE SORRY.

THAVES 3-29
© 1988 by NEA, Inc.

gelists continually reinforce this negative perception by their hucksterism and personal lifestyles.

From the sitcoms to the soaps to the cartoons to the movies, religion is for laughs . . . as is living by the Mosaic yardstick of behavior. That fell by the wayside long ago, with the demise of *Dragnet* and *Hawaii Five-O*. Today there is such a blurring of the lines between good and evil that it is virtually impossible to find positive role models in more than rare isolated cases.

Famed playwright Loring Mandel declared: "I believe that the great droning, giggling body of television is polluting us. . . . Most of television betrays us. It lies about what this world is like and what it means to be human. . . . Children spend perhaps twice as much time being educated by television as by school. . . . The problem is, it mostly teaches lies" ("How I'd Save Television," *Parade*, May 11, 1986).

Tom Shales offered this sobering critique of today's television: "For years, for centuries, a primary theme of literature and theater was the struggle between good and evil. Until the seventies and Watergate, this was also a dominant theme of television fare."

But today? Shales notes that "when popular entertainment abandons the concepts of good and evil, is it also abdicating the role in portraying the difference between right and wrong? People tuning in to prime-time TV . . . do not see right conquering wrong. To the contrary, they see villains treated as heroes. . . . If these programs are a response to moral confusion rather than a contributor to it, their proliferation nevertheless helps perpetuate the idea that right and wrong are outmoded commodities, that the wages of sin amount mainly to money, power, and glamour" ("There's No Good 'Evil' Found on TV Anymore," Fort Worth *Star-Telegram*, June 29, 1982).

Decades ago Chinese leader Chiang Kai-shek warned us what such a condition means: "No matter whether it be an individual or a nation, the loss of integrity is tantamount to death itself."

David Kucharsky warned, "Viewers should be most wary of situation comedies. Their subtle put-downs of Christian sexual standards are devastating, especially to teens and smaller children. Many of our youth feel that about the worst thing that can happen to them is to be laughed at" (*Christian Herald*, Sept. 1978).

New York *Post* TV editor Paul Dennis, in his recent *Favorite Families of TV*, postulates that it is just not true at all that early family shows were untrue to life, or were saccharine

"Many social analysts are convinced that TV has moved ahead of home, church, and school as the principal influence on morality. What these children see is wholesale assaults on traditional values, extensive drug and alcohol use and abuse, violence, sex, greed and gambling" (Steve Allen, U.S. News & World Report, Oct. 13, 1975).

in their portrayals: "The best family shows all did it . . . One member went out of sync, then was shamed back into sync. That was our lesson. That's how it was supposed to work.

"Not perfection. Imperfection and forgiveness.

"Then *All in the Family* came along and everything changed, until today we have a kind of reverse Fascism. There's no such thing as a family where you get out of sync, then come back in. There are exceptions, of course, *The Cosby Show* is like *Father Knows Best* in Black face. Families such as the Bundies or the Simpsons are so dysfunctional it's like they are beating us over the head with it" (cited in David Hinckley, "New Book's Conclusion: American TV Families Worked Best in the Fifties," *The Capital*, May 13, 1992).

TV's soaps are one of television's chief miseducators, with their steady diet of abnormal and immoral lives—all dominated by sexuality. Marriage is only a stage—an arrangement—that will last out, perhaps, only the sexual high; when that peaks and begins to wane, it will be time to move on—no matter the heartbreak of spouse and children left behind. In today's media, including popular music, "love" brings with it no responsibilities to people, and embodies the long-term commitment of a rabbit.

The act of loving someone is changed by the media from something beautiful (a God-given gift that cements a home and results in commit-

> *"We may have fewer complexes since sex became liberated, but we also have less of the beauty of sexual life. The romance is gone"* (George Plagenz, "Sex and Morality Difficult to Define," Fort Worth Star-Telegram, May 25, 1982).

ment and determination to be there for life as your children grow up, as their children grow up, and as your spouse ages and loses youthful appearance) to a hedonistic James Bond playboyism—that sex is all in all and that genuine caring for one's sex partners is a laugh. When the thrill is gone, move on to the next thrill . . . and the next. All relationships in life are throw away and one-night-standish, and people who expect lifetime commitment are fools.

George Plagenz observed that "situation ethics has rewritten the commandment on adultery so that it reads: 'Thou shalt not commit adultery—ordinarily.' . . . In its original and unrevised form, however, the commandment against adultery was not intended to come to terms with human nature. Its purpose was the humanized nature—to set a high but not unattainable standard which would help mankind resist the downward pull of brute nature. Its practiced benefit would be to preserve the inviolability of the home on which civilization—if not human nature—rests" ("Sex and Morality Difficult to Define," Forth Worth *Star-Telegram*, May 25, 1982).

Plagenz then turned to another aspect of media miseducation: "Our society seems to have removed premarital sex and sex between unmarried people from the area of morality. But we are paying a high price for our indulgence in casual sex. The novelist D. H. Lawrence warned 50 years ago that 'a too free intimacy between the sexes is sterilizing; it makes neuters. Later on, no deep, magical sex life is possible' " (*ibid.*).

As I counsel with students and adults, I frankly admit to them that it is mighty tough to hold a marriage relationship together for a lifetime. It takes much effort and a willingness to adapt to your partner's journey and personal dreams continually, to stay together and be there for your children and grandchildren through all the tribulations, misunderstandings, and heartbreak life brings. This commitment to seeing a relationship through, for life, is possible only with the good Lord's help.

What some of them tell me is just how devastating the media's "love 'em and leave 'em" philosophy of life can be when translated into the reality of their everyday lives: to give an individual your heart and then see it trampled on. The leaving itself is oftentimes not as painful as the turning on and off 'like a faucet' of caring love, of the lack of concern for those who once constituted a family during the long years of separation lying ahead. For the children, it's like a trapdoor was slammed. It is this sense of abandonment, this shriveling up of one's concept of self-worth, that constitutes such an American tragedy.

And its implications ripple on and on throughout life. Some years ago, while I directed Southwestern's Adult Degree Program, I was asked a question that ended up changing my life. It was asked by a woman whose parents had divorced during the early years of her childhood: "Dr. Wheeler, are you my friend until I graduate . . . or are you my friend for the long haul?" She knew that I was paid for seeing her through to the degree—what she really wanted to know, before she dared to open very wide the door of friendship, was whether or not my interest in her as a person had an expiration date stamped on it. Our society is so saturated with planned obsolescence, divorce, and one-night stands, that she wanted to know if I represented merely the society norm or one of those all-too-rare incidents in contemporary American life: offering to be a lifelong friend.

That question made me reevaluate every last relationship in my life at that time. Even more significantly, it raised friendship and being there for others to the number one priority for the rest of my life.

Quietly, without fanfare, during the past four decades the media have all but destroyed the American soul. Those traditional bulwarks, the home, school, and church, have surrendered their roles without a whimper. But we can't say we haven't been warned! During these same years a huge body of scholarship has been churned out, and it has been widely reported in the secular and religious press. Their findings? Almost universally negative! And they have consistently prophesied what has now come to pass.

Former Secretary of Education William Bennett declared to New York's Harvard Club: "If we want our children to possess the traits of character we most admire, we need to teach them what those traits are. They must learn to identify the forms and contents of those traits. They must achieve at least a minimal level of moral literacy that

"Parents don't have the sense to use the off button. . . . No television show, no matter how marvelous, can compete (in value) with the time of the parent if the parent wants to communicate. . . . Most of the parents in this country do not seem to care about the time spent or the programs being viewed by their young people. The most often spoken words in America today are not 'I love you,' 'You did well at that,' or 'That's not so bad, go back and try again, you can do it.' No, the most often spoken words we hear in America today are 'I'm busy, so watch television' " (cited in William Gildea, "Captain Kangaroo Cites TV for Communication Gap," Washington Post, 1977; italics supplied).

will enable them to make sense of what they see in life, and, we may hope, that will help them live it well. Instead . . . we have overintellectualized character instruction virtually out of existence" (1986 Associated Press news release).

Columnist William Raspberry, commenting on Bennett's speech in a 1986 column, warned that moral growth cannot be expected to occur in a "moral vacuum." As for our media, it has been worse than a moral vacuum: it has clearly and systematically dismantled society's pre-TV moral didacticism.

Current scholarship reveals that members of today's average family communicate with each other only 14 minutes a day, and the average father communicates with each child 42 *seconds a day!* On the other hand, the TV set is on in our homes *seven hours and five minutes each day!*

The late Michael Landon, in one of his last interviews, observed: "When it gets to the point where my lads can learn more on TV than by reading history or philosophy, then they can watch television. Families don't talk together anymore—and that's an American tragedy."

Early in 1983, columnist Sydney Harris condemned television for rather strange reasons, calling the media "an expense of spirit in a waste of shame. . . . Millions of man- and woman-hours [are] expended on charades, unworthy of their multifaceted talents" ("Television Wastes Talents," Fort Worth *Star-Telegram,* Jan. 13, 1983).

"Who is the most prolific and tireless story teller in your home? It used to be the parent, grandparent, or older sibling. Today, in most homes it is television—by far. Television has achieved what all emperors and popes could only dream about: a pulpit in every living room, with a charismatic messenger providing a common ritual of entertainment and information with a central underlying sales message to all" (George Gerbner, "Television Most Popular Storyteller in Today's Culture," Fort Worth Star-Telegram, Feb. 5, 1978).

Morgan Gendel's first words in a 1986 Los Angeles *Times* article on television were: " 'Audible wallpaper' is how one scholar once referred to television, a reference to the ceaseless drone of mind-numbing fare that emanates from the ubiquitous tube" ("Different Pulpits, Same Message—Beware TV," Los Angeles *Times,* Feb. 18, 1986).

In the mid-1960s the Association for Childhood Education International published one of the most significant studies ever done on television. At that time the medium was not quite 20 years old; thus knowledge of television's impact was still in relative infancy. Nevertheless, some of the findings generated by years of study proved to be provocative indeed. One of the study editors, Ralph Garry of Boston University, warned that "although it is not until the age of 6 or 7 that a child can make much sense out of a film story, scattered evidence indicates that the very young child has enough contact with sound and image to be emotionally vulnerable. Reacting to isolated episodes, the young child gets no relief from the context, and his emotions are often intense because of the 'all or none' fashion in which he responds emotionally" (*Children and TV*, [1967]).

> *"Children are sensitive to what they see happening to children in other programs, particularly those of similar age and sex. In contrast, they often completely miss the point of the adult interactions which they see on television" (Ralph Garry, ibid.).*

Betty Longstreet and Frank Orme of the National Association for Better Broadcasting make some of the most significant observations that have ever been written on the subject of TV: "Unlike adults, children do not put education in one category and entertainment in another. A child learns from *everything he sees*. He learns not so much from what people tell him as from what he sees them actually doing. To a child, the television world is peopled by real people. He sees mothers and fathers and children—persons readily recognizable as part of his real environment. He is not equipped to distinguish between fantasy and reality, or between acceptable and nonacceptable models, of conduct" (*ibid.* italics supplied).

✦ ✦ ✦

Side by Side

They lie on the table, side by side:
The Holy Bible and the *TV Guide*.
One is well worn, but cherished with pride.
(Not the Bible, but the *TV Guide*.)

As the pages are turned, what shall they see?
Oh, what does it matter, turn on the TV.
Then confusion reigns; they can't all agree
On what they shall watch on the old TV.
So they open the book in which they confide.
(No! Not the Bible: it's the *TV Guide*.)

The Word of God is seldom read.
Maybe a verse e'er they fall into bed
Exhausted and sleepy and tired as can be.
Not from reading the Bible; from watching TV.

So then, back to the table, side by side,
Lie the Holy Bible and the *TV Guide*.
No time for prayer, no time for the Word.
The plan of salvation is seldom heard.
But forgiveness of sin so full and free
Is found in the Bible, not on TV!

Author Unknown

CHAPTER 11

The Long Bloody Trail— Violence in America

Before television, to put it mildly, we were a different people. We were, generally speaking, law-abiding, peaceable, strong believers in God and country, solidly honest, generous to a fault, and devout believers in the Puritan work ethic (that hard work was both God-ordained and expected of *everyone*).

To capsulize it all in a few words: it was a good world in which to live. . . and unlocked houses were the norm. Neighbors wandered in and out of each other's houses; when someone was in trouble on the road—or anywhere else, for that matter!—you stopped to help; when someone knocked on your door, he or she was invited in (on the frontier, if your worst enemy asked for hospitality for the night, you were morally obliged to grant the request); also, on the frontier, most contracts were based merely on handshakes—yet the default rate was virtually zero: defaults and bankruptcies came much later—with the lawyers.

"THAT DOES IT! I'M NOT GOING TO ALLOW YOU KIDS TO WATCH ALL THAT VIOLENCE ON T.V. ANYMORE!
Ed Gamble/Register & Tribune Syndicate
Reprinted with special permission of King Features Syndicate.

Of course there were exceptions—there always have been . . . but that's what they were: exceptions.

All this changed with the advent of television and the mass media. Not overnight but gradually—and not a very slow gradually at that: but one generation took us to the Rubicon years of the 60s where, in but five short years, assassins' bullets cut down in the prime of their lives John F. Kennedy, Malcolm X, Martin Luther King, Jr., and Robert Kennedy. . . . We have not been the same since. The next generation took us to today: the bloodiest society on earth.

But it took a major study to re-

Crumbling is not an instant's Act
A fundamental pause
Dilapidation's processes
Are organized Decays.

'Tis first a Cobweb on the Soul
A Cuticle of Dust
A Borer in the Axis
An Elemental Rust—

Ruin is formal—Devil's work
Consecutive and slow—
Fall in an instant, no man did
Slipping—is Crash's Law.
—Emily Dickinson

veal to me (in slow motion) the stages of our fall—and the horrifying society that replaced what we once were. The key serendipitous moment in the evolution of this book occurred when the urge came upon me to arrange all the clippings, articles, columns, and studies, dealing with violence through the years—not thematically but chronologically, by date published. Only *then* did it all come into focus for me. As I started reading, in sequence, I hadn't gone very far before I realized that something totally unexpected was happening: before my eyes, not only was I seeing a retelling of the history of this country but I was also seeing, parallel, a sociological history, with our changing mores clearly chronicled. I was seeing—like a negative gradually coming into focus in a darkroom developing tray—the steady intensification of violence and the corresponding numbing of the American soul. By the time I got to the mid-80s, the case against television and what its purveyors were doing to us as a people was so overwhelming that I wanted to quit right there—I just didn't want to see any more. But I forced myself to continue. By the time I got to 1992, what I was reading froze my blood. . . . Following are a few of these crucial milestones.

But first, let's utilize Eric F. Goldman's summation of what we were as a people on the eve of television's arrival on the American stage:

"We are a people whose history has made us the land of the swift, total solution, brought about by ourselves alone. We faced a wilderness; we hacked it down. We were vexed by slavery; we cut it out of our system. We fought Britishers, Mexicans, Spaniards, Germans, Germans plus Japanese, and licked them all with short shrift. No wonder our movies have a happy ending, and in ninety minutes. No wonder we are the only country in the world which has produced a popular saying like: 'The difficult we do immediately, the impossible takes a little time' " (Goldman, *The Crucial Decade—and After,* Vintage Books, New York, 1960).

1957   Charles Van Doren, for week after week, had mesmerized TV listeners with his riveting performances as a contestant in the hit NBC program "Twenty One." When it was revealed that it had all been a sham, the nation reeled with the shock of it.

Why? According to Goldman, "moral relativism" had replaced "moral certitude" and "brought in its wake moral lassitude and confusion."

1959   So great was the outcry that two years later, *Look* magazine editors sent out a 12-member team of investigating reporters to criss-cross the country polling people everywhere to see if we as a people really had changed. What did they find? They found a new code of ethics emerging: "Whatever you do is all right if it's legal or if you disapprove of the law. It's all right if it doesn't hurt anybody. And it's all right if it's part of accepted business practices" (Goldman, p. 324).

John Steinbeck, wracked and tormented by what he was seeing, wrote his friend Adlai Stevenson, saying, ". . . a creeping, all-pervading, nerve gas of immorality starts in the nursery and does not stop before it reaches the highest office, both corporate and governmental. . . . On all levels American society is rigged. . . . I am troubled by the cynical immorality of my country. It cannot survive on this basis" (Goldman, p. 325).

Dr. Harold Shryock quoted Dr. Lawrence Kubie, Yale University professor, who warned that "the constant confrontation with killing, bloodletting in a form so realistic that to a child it's as real as life itself" would most certainly leave a frightening legacy in its wake ("Children and Television," *Review and Herald,* Apr. 2, 1959).

1964   Kitty Genovese was stabbed to death on a Queens, New York, street while 38 witnesses in the apartment house she was seeking safety in watched the long drawn-out and brutal attack—and *did nothing!* The story flashed across the country in hours, and Americans recoiled in disbelief at what they were becoming: at such criminal callousness.

1973   In October, six Boston youth forced a Swiss-born woman to pour gasoline all over herself—and then set her afire. Police angrily blamed the atrocity on the just-televised (48 hours before) human torch scene in the movie *Fuzz.* The torch murder caused such an outcry that *U.S. News & World Report* ran a cover story on it; according to its report, "The television industry insists that there is no solid evidence that violence on TV spawns crime and violence in society." However, it was noted that in a recent University of Pennsylvania study, it was discovered that "Half of all people on TV commit violence, one fifth perpetrate some crime, 6% kill someone. . . ." As for the perceived effects on children, "TV programmers continue to deny complicity: 'If TV violence causes violence it is only in those disturbed people who already have a propensity toward violence,' contends one network programmer in New York City. 'We know that some people who watch TV violence are comforted by the fact that it's not happening to them. They feel vicariously released and lucky' " ("Violence on TV: Why People Are Upset," *U.S. News & World Report,* Oct. 29, 1973).

About five weeks later, Shana Alexander (of *Newsweek*) entered into the fray; she wrote: "Constant exposure of children to explicit violence on movies and TV has a damaging, dulling, blunting effect on their sensibilities. People know this instinctively. That's why two thirds of Americans say there is too much violence on TV. . . . What I hate to see, and I myself walk out of, is the aimless, brainless, sexual violence in pictures. . . . What shocks me is the sudden ugly prevalence of rape scenes—20 in recent months. As a sexual turn-on, the rape scene has replaced the obligatory movie bubble bath of the 1930s. I agree with critic Aljean Harmetz that the attack between the thighs is only an extension of the bullet between the eyes.

"We can and must suppress the brutality which another age will recognize as the one common hallmark of all our commercial entertainment. Kids' cartoons, pro football, the nightly news, all TV drama, and all movies now reek with sadism and gratuitous gore" ("Hanging Out in Sexual Space," *Newsweek,* Nov. 12, 1973).

1975   According to a Nielsen survey, on a recent week-day evening, between 10 and 11 p.m., there were still 5 million kids glued to the set.

In March, *Newsweek* reporters observed that "Certainly TV entertainment has never been so violent. Twenty years ago, 'action-adventure programming' (a cherished network euphemism for shoot-em-ups) accounted for less than 20% of all prime-time offerings. Today that figure has soared to 60%, propelled by no fewer than 24 current crime series. . . . Now, no less influential figure than CBS president Arthur Taylor, who first proposed the family hour concept, allows that TV is increasingly one of the probable determinants of antisocial behavior" ("Drop That Gun, Captain Video,"

Newsweek, Mar. 10, 1975).

It was in the December 8 issue of the prestigious *Journal of the American Medical Association* that one of the biggest guns entered into the fray. The author of the study, Dr. Michael B. Rothenberg (of Seattle's Children's Orthopedic Hospital and the University of Washington School of Medicine), unleased such a barrage of data and findings that it made news around the country. He called for an organized cry from the medical profession against violence on television and its effects on children, noting that 25 years of investigation of the relationship of television violence to aggressive behavior in children — research spawned by 146 articles in science journals, representing 50 studies involving 10,000 children and adolescents from every conceivable background — *conclusively showed that viewing violence produced aggressive behavior in the young.*

Rothenberg further noted that an estimated 200,000,000 guns in the U.S., averaging out to one for almost every man, woman, and child in the country, are now in circulation. A new hand gun is sold every 13 seconds and used ones traded at the rate of one every 30 seconds. And 5,000,000 new ones are churned out every year. And the result? Every four minutes someone is killed or wounded by gunfire. Every three minutes someone is robbed at gunpoint.

Rothenberg also revealed that the reason why the controversial 1972 Surgeon General's Report was so waffling was that the "Television industry representatives 'blackballed' the seven of the 40 listed scientists who had the most outstanding reputations and work in the field of violence research" — they were replaced with television network executives.

And, for good measure, he noted that there is six times more violence during one hour of children's television than there is in one hour of adult television *(The Journal of the American Medical Association,* Dec. 8, 1975).

1976   Between 1960 and 1974, the annual homicide rate in the U.S. rose more than 100%. In 1975, more than 20,000 Americans were murdered. The death rate for 15- to 24-year-olds alone rose 19% between 1961 and 1974. According to Delores Katz, sociologists and psychiatrists agree that television violence is a major contributing factor to violence on our streets; this was confirmed by the final report made by the National Commission on the Causes and Prevention of Violence in 1969 ("Homicide Fastest Growing Cause of Death," Delores Katz, Fort Worth *Star-Telegram*).

Late in August, FBI statistics for the year went out over the wires. They revealed that, in an average hour in 1975, 2 were murdered, 6 women were raped, 56 were assaulted, 52 were robbed, 112 vehicles were stolen, 360 burglaries were committed, and 720 persons or businesses became victims of larceny. Put together: "a river of numbers gone mad: 56,000 forcible rapes, 484,710 aggravated assaults, 20,510 murders, 3.25 million burglaries. The numbers are numbing. . . . And 15,000 reported cases of child abuse" (Kate Sherrod, Fort Worth *Star-Telegram*, Aug. 29, 1976).

1977   In February, a congressional panel released staggering figures dealing with violence in schools. 600 million dollars was spent in '75 alone as a result of vandalism (more than enough money to hire 50,000 more teachers!). Even more alarming were the 70,000 serious assaults on teachers and the hundreds of thousands of attacks on students. These assaults increased 58% during '70 to '74; sex offenses, 62%; drug-related crimes, 81%; and robbery up 117%! ("Panel Reports Violence in Schools Increasing to Shocking Proportions," Fort Worth *Star-Telegram*, Feb. 26, 1977).

Only one day later, another report revealed that "For more than 5 million children, punishment at home has meant being shot, stabbed, kicked, beaten and bitten by parents. . . . Three out of every 100 parents, an estimated 1.2 million parents nationwide, have used knives or guns on their children. . . . It is estimated that there are about 700 deaths a year of children who die from home violence. . . . 28% of couples surveyed admitted to slapping or hitting each other. . . . 1% had shot, stabbed, or severely beaten the partner" (Fort Worth *Star-Telegram,* Feb. 27, 1977).

In September of '77, another crime made national headlines: "Dolphus Thompson, 14, shot and killed his brother, in imitation of how it was done in a Clint Eastwood film, *Dirty Harry.* Joseph Di Leonardi, commander of the homicide division of the Chicago police . . . said there's no question about it . . . seeing these things on television brings out the aggression in young people. Children of that age are very impressionable. They imitate characters they see on TV. *This violence infects* the children's minds. I see it every day. We ask a youngster where he got the idea to commit a certain kind of act of violence, and he says, 'I saw it on *Baretta,* or 'I saw it on the TV movie.' . . . When I heard that *Dirty Harry* was going to be shown on TV again, I thought, 'Oh no!' " Also noted was the sequel to that movie: *Magnum Force*—in it, there are 39 murders in 120 minutes (Bob Greene, "Viewing TV Hazardous to Health," Fort Worth *Star-Telegram,* Sept. 1977).

"Much of the misery of this life is caused by being unkind to those who love us" (George F. Hoffman).

Only weeks later, the trial of 15-year-old Ronny Zamora was used by *Newsweek* to highlight the problem even more: "Ignored or beaten at home, the boy spent six hours a day in front of the TV set . . . with 'the only friends he had, *Kojak, Baretta,* and *Police Woman.*" Zamora and a teenage pal broke into a neighbor's house where Zamora murdered an 82-year-old woman with his pistol. Zamora's lawyer, Ellis Rubin, entered a plea of not guilty by insanity; a steady dose of TV violence, the lawyer argued, made it impossible for the boy to tell right from wrong" ("The Trials of TV," *Newsweek,* Oct. 10, 1977).

1978   Early in 1978, George Gerbner warned his readers that "We have to make a distinction between violence that is selectively used, violence that is handcrafted to show its tragic consequences, to show the pain and to show the suffering and tragedy that follows. That's

> *"We all become like that with which we live, like that which we look upon, read, or hear" (William F. Stidger).*

not what we are talking about. We're talking about mass-produced, cheap, industrial violence that's injected into every home whether they like it or not" ("Television Most Popular Storyteller in Today's Culture," Fort Worth *Star-Telegram,* Feb. 5, 1978).

1979   Robert Fulton and Eric Markusen, in a thoughtful discussion of how death is portrayed in popular culture, noted that "Unlike in real life, Prime-time television shows murder and mayhem relentlessly, while portraying only superficially the human qualities of the victims." After excoriating the gratuitous violence and gore in television and in movies, the authors observed that "children who have never attended a funeral or seen a corpse have seen thousands of killings on television. Most of us know more about how to kill another person than how to treat the dying or comfort the bereaved. . . . Such desentization can have dangerous consequences if it hinders us from taking actual death seriously. We are reminded of the tragic case of Kitty Genovese, who was stabbed to death near her home while neighbors listened to her screams with apparent indifference" ("Death in Popular Culture," Burleson *Star,* Feb. 2, 1979).

1980   Early in 1980, in Texas there was a symposium conducted by experts on violence; their frame of reference was the previous 20 years. Dr. Carol Nadelson declared, on rape, that "It is not sexual desire. It is an act of aggression. Incidents of rape have increased 200% in 10 years," she said. Nadelson blames, in part, the "slide into permissiveness. People are excused from having to deal with their impulses; they aren't taught to act within certain boundaries of human behavior" ("Violence in America (1960-1980)," Fort Worth *Star-Telegram,* Feb. 14, 1980).

According to Dr. Ronald Slaby, in research at the University of Washington, the following are lessons likely to be learned by watching TV violence:

"1. Violence is rampant.

2. Violence works.

3. Violence is frequently rewarded.

4. Violence is often justifiable.

5. Violence is clean.

6. Violence is often funny.

7. Violence is often done just for the fun of it.

8. Violence is sometimes done in new and unique ways.

9. Violence is more appropriate for males than for females.

10. Violence is something to be watched, tolerated, and even entertained by" ("Wrong Lessons Learned From TV," cited by Lula T. Sanford and Ann Felter, Fort Worth *Star-Telegram,* n.d.).

1984   Clark Warren approached violence via the emotion of anger: "While anger is the most powerful and dangerous of our emotions, no one is ever trained how to handle it. The way the anger is modeled by the media, especially television and the movies, is to handle it immediately, usually in an explosive way with guns or knives or cars or fists or a tongue lashing. Kids watch that four or five hours a day, and how can we expect them to act differently when they get angry? Anger management is a skill and you have to work at it" *(Sunshine Magazine,* June 1984).

1985   In January of 1985, columnist Bob Greene returned to the attack: "The point is television violence is a terrible pollutant. TV is the most powerful medium of communication in history, and what it does is bring act after act of awful violence into our homes. It has become an intruder. . . . In 1982 it was reported that an average of eight violent acts per hour occurred on network prime-time television—and a year later it was reported that 300% more violent acts occurred on the pay-movie cable channels than on the network. . . . The sickening fact is that the people who program network television have decided that a perfectly acceptable way to entertain Americans is to show them televised pictures of people wounding and killing other people. . . . Clearly the life that is portrayed on television is based on the meanest and sickest levels of society. The placid, gentle parts of society don't get mirrored much" ("Television Polluting Our Homes With Violence," (*Rocky Mountain News,* Jan. 25, 1985).

1989   Only occasionally in our shell-shocked nation does a single act of crime elicit more than a shrug. One exception was the 1989 "Wilding" incident in New York City's Central Park. So brutal and senseless was the gang rape of an attractive and caring young Yale graduate that even the nation's media recoiled in horror. More than 30 youngsters (most under 16) participated in the rape/attack: assaulting the jogger with a pipe, hacking her skull and thighs with a knife, pounding her face with a brick. "Why?" asked everyone. George Will tagged it with a word seldom used by today's media—"evil."

Mary McGrory put it this way: "Obviously, their parents, their schools, did not tell them about the golden rule. Television, with its verbal and physical violence, its depiction of sex as an instantly available right, its boorish hosts and witless guests, certainly didn't teach them. . . . It is to weep" ("Horror in the Park," Washington *Post,* Apr. 30, 1989).

About the same time as the Wilding attack, 15-year-old Michael Thomas was murdered by 17-year-old James Martin. Motive for the murder: Thomas' $115 Nike Air Jordan tennis shoes. Tom Marquards, Annapolis *The Capital* editor, musing about the senseless sacrifice of a life, noted that in recent months, a D.C. student was murdered for a jacket; and locally, another student was slain for his Honda motorcycle.

So Marquardt asked Annapolis psychologist Tom Muha *Why?* "There is a breakdown of the family," declared Muha. "Kids are coming from divorced families and often it's the mother who is raising the kids. It's a heavy-duty load for a mother and moms are not traditionally authoritarian. . . . New studies show that 62% of marriages end in divorce. . . . With only one parent at home, how can children get the discipline and the value system so important to their transition into adulthood?"

Marquardt wrapped up his column with this counsel: "There's nothing unhealthy about emulating heroes, but kids murdering kids for tennis shoes and jackets sends a chill down our spine. It's not going to change until parents accept the responsibility of the children's future. Only when people start to think about the consequences of divorce, the consequences of single-parent child rearing, and the consequences of a neglected child will we see a return to a less violent society. If you have a marriage, maintain it. If you have children, teach them" ("Two Boys in Different Worlds Meet Violently Over Shoes," *The Capital,* May 14, 1989).

Richard Cohen used the Wilding atrocity as a vehicle of reference in a May column. Sadly concluding that just as the crime reveals that none of us are safe anymore anywhere, it also makes some of us compare now to what once was. Cohen suggested raising from the dead a mythical grandfather and showing him the here and now: "Read him the papers and show him television and then take him for a walk. . . . I would say, as we walk, that in the last year my apartment was burglarized in Washington and my car stolen in New York. In Washington, the school board plans to put metal detectors in schools so weapons can be detected and taken away from students. In New York, signs in car windows say 'no radio.' . . . Their owners spent $60,000 and up for them, yet for all that, they can't even have a radio. . . . To get into my office in Washington, I must show a building pass. . . . Now you have to have an elevator pass, a card to insert into a slot to inform the elevator that you are friendly. . . . But think of the industry of crime. Can we calculate the cost of it? Crime prevention must be America's No. 1 industry. What is the cost of security guards, metal detectors, added police, the jails? What is the cost of the paranoid elevator that won't let you up? . . . What is the total cost of window

> *Courtland Milloy, noting the fact that twice as many Black men are in prison as are in college, explained it thus:*
> *"A psychological battle is . . . being waged against black men . . . that relies heavily on the mass media to perpetrate demoralizing myths and stereotypes.*
> *Jawanza Kunjufu, author of 'Countering the Conspiracy to Destroy Black Boys,' agrees. The role models that have seized the imagination of so many black youth are gangs, drug dealers, convicts, athletes and comedians as portrayed in the press and on television" (Courtland Milloy, "Liberating Young Men From Maleness", Washington Post, Feb. 17, 1993).*

bars and reinforced doors, of muscled-up locks and security systems? . . . And what is the psychic cost? If I am told that worrying can cost me years off my life, then what is the cost of constantly worrying about crime?" Thinking back to the flowers he saw on the spot where the savaged jogger was found, Cohen poignantly asks the question: "What are we mourning—the woman who was brutalized on that spot, or the way things once were? A flower for her. A bouquet for us all" ("Crimes and the Heart," Washington *Post,* May 21, 1989).

1990   According to the Washington *Post,* deregulation of the television industry 10 years ago has not been a good thing: "Since deregulation in 1980, children's programs that featured about 18.6 violent acts per hour now have about 26.4 violent acts per hour." Adult programming has remained at about 16 violent acts per hour ("For Children's TV, Increased Violence," Washington *Post,* Feb. 1990).

Later in the year, Alan Mirabella wondered to what depths the movie industry would stoop in order to make a buck. He noted that "While the summer's films are chock full of violence by larger-than-life characters, many film critics and a watchdog group are disturbed that *RoboCop 2* features kids as the purveyors of mayhem—depictions they feel demonstrate how extreme screen violence has become." . . . "There is an escalating level of sadism on the screen," says Chicago *Tribune* critic David Kehr. "And when a filmmaker uses children—traditionally a symbol of innocence—you see how extreme violence has become" ("Robo-Cop's Murderous Kids Escalate Debate Over Violence," *The Capital,* July 9, 1990).

Late in December, Richard Cohen again took up the subject of violence and crime in America. He compared what things were like in 1964 when Kitty Genovese was stabbed to death in New York to conditions in 1990, 26 years later: "The year Kitty Genovese was killed, New York's murder rate was 6.1 per 100,000. In 1989 it was 22.7. Washington's record is even more alarming: from 8.4 in 1964 to 59.5 in 1988 and climbing. Back in 1964 your average murder was a domestic affair—husbands, wives, lovers, and a few of them (19 percent in 1960) involved guns. Now strangers kill strangers, and most often (66 percent last year in New York) guns were involved. Crimes of passion have become crimes of dispassion.

"But even apart from guns—the sheer number of them—is the willingness to use them, to kill. Knives or

THE LONG BLOODY TRAIL—VIOLENCE IN AMERICA

guns, it matters not. The taking of a life is nothing. Cops are numbed by the cold cruelty of children. Each year, Washington careens from one homicide record to another, too much of it attributable to kids. . . . Now city dwellers are like people in Nazi-occupied Europe. The terror is so great that we tend to suspend moral judgment. . . . Notions of accountability, of what is owed others, no longer apply. In their place is the credo of the city dweller: Mind your own business. . . . The greatest military and economic power on Earth can't keep a girl safe on the subway" ("Crimes of Dispassion," Washington *Post*, Dec. 21, 1990).

1991   The crime reports for the year end, on January 9, William Raspberry of the Washington *Post* noted that the violence that is sweeping across America is sadly reflected in Washington: "703 homicides [up from the 400's only two years ago]." Raspberry urged his readers to take it upon themselves to teach young people that killing is wrong. For they certainly won't get that instruction from the media for they "routinely exalt violence" ("Teach Three R's Plus One," Washington *Post*, Jan. 9, 1991).

A month later, George Will called attention to a society out of control. He pointed out that in New York alone there are today 2,200 homicides a year, as compared to 292 in 1945! 100,000 cases of armed robbery (about one every five minutes) as compared to 1,417 in 1945—and today there are 390 car thefts a day! As for reasons, Will observed, "For more than a generation, the fundamental act of American fun—watching television—has involved, for the average viewer, seeing 150 acts of violence and 15 murders a week. Is it really amazing that life seems to have been cheapened?" ("What Grandmother Took for Granted," Washington *Post*, Feb. 14, 1991).

1992   A February Associated Press release had to do with increasingly horrifying crimes, more often than not committed on the pettiest of pretexts. "More and more we see criminals who are willing to use lethal force if necessary.... FBI statistics show the incidence of violent crimes ... has climbed by 18% during the past five years. Much of that increase is drug-related, and officials also blame other factors—violence on television and the movies and the disintegration of societal restraints" ("Increasingly Horrifying Crimes Worry Authorities," Washington *Post*, Feb. 15, 1992).

In April, there appeared in the Washington *Post* a landmark article on television titled "Primal Screen" by Don Oldenburg. He pointed out that crime, instead of leveling off or going down—just keeps getting worse and worse: "Justice figures showing the youth arrest rate for murder, manslaughter, forcible rape, robbery, and aggravated assault increased by 16 percent between 1989 and 1990 [in only *one* *year!*]."

"Shame on Hollywood for an endless stream of films filled with profanity, nudity, sex, violence and killings. For example, the giant hit Basic Instinct features murders during orgasms, setting a new standard of perversion even for today's movies" (Donald E. Wildmon ad, "We Are Outraged!" Washington Post, Feb. 21, 1993).

Oldenburg then moved on to a just-released major study ("Big World, Small Screen"), conducted by the American Psychological Association, and 5 years in the making. The findings confirmed earlier suppositions: the child who watches 2 to 4 hours of TV a day will have witnessed 8,000 murders and 100,000 other acts of violence *before* leaving elementary school.

Oldenburg also discussed in depth the findings of Dr. Leonard Eron of the University of Illinois. Dr. Eron's study is considered major because it spans over three decades and chronicles the lives of the same people. In it, for the first time there was conclusive proof of the staying power of TV imagery: although he found little relation to what one watched at age 19 and how aggressive one was at age 30, what was truly frightening was this:

The more hours of television the children watched when they were 8 years old . . . the more serious were the crimes they were convicted of by the time they were age 30, and the more aggressive they were under the influence of alcohol, and the more severely they punished their own children.

According to this 30-year study, the most risky age for TV violence is during the first 10 years of a child's life. "Until children reach the double digits," says Eron, "they find it very difficult to differentiate between what's real and what's not real on TV" ("Primal Screen," Washington *Post*, Apr. 7, 1992).

In the June 10 issue of *Journal of the American Medical Association,* the proverbial smoking gun was finally found so that it could be introduced in the case against TV as conclusive evidence. *According to Dr. Centerwall of the University of Washington, television is directly responsible for 10,000 homicides, 70,000 rapes, and 700,000 injurious assaults every year—roughly about half of all serious crimes.* According to Dr. Centerwall's long postulated theory: 10 to 15 years after a society embraces television, expect a dramatic increase in murders and other serious crimes. That's just enough time, he notes, for the first generation weaned on television to reach adulthood and move into their most crime-prone years. He first noted it in the case of the U.S. and Canada, but thought maybe the fulfillment of his postulate might have been a fluke. However, television did not become prevalent in South Africa—because of strong government controls—until 1974. So it was that, as the years passed, he watched South Africa with baited breath. But sure enough, about 10 to 15 years later, South Africa's murder rate soared 56 percent! (counting only crimes committed by Whites against Whites). . . . Thanks to Centerwall's study, there can no longer remain any doubt: *television embodies in itself the blood-*

iest killing machine ever devised by the hand of man!

Centerwall also, in that same issue, demolished another myth: that babies don't absorb much from what they see on television. Drawing from a landmark study by A. N. Meltzoff, he used actual photographs of a 14-month-old infant taken in a test situation to prove his point:

"In photograph A the adult pulls apart a novel toy. The infant leans forward and carefully studies the adult's actions.

"In photograph B the infant is given the toy.

"In photograph C the infant pulls the toy apart, imitating what he had seen the adult do.

"Of infants exposed to the instructional video, 65% could later work the toy, as compared to 20% of the unexposed infants."

Clearly, with this degree of retention and awareness, it is not safe to leave even infants in the vicinity of a television set which is on.

Turning to another issue, Centerwall observed rather wryly that it is unrealistic to expect the tobacco industry and television to operate altruistically for the best good of consumers, noting that "Cable aside, the television industry is not in the business of selling programs to audiences. It is in the business of selling audiences to advertisers. Issues of 'quality' and 'social responsibility' are entirely peripheral to the issue of maximizing audience size within a competitive market—and there is no formula more tried and true than violence for reliably generating large audiences that can be sold to advertisers. . . . For this reason, industry spokespersons have made innumerable protestations of good intent, but nothing has happened. In over 20 years of monitoring levels of television violence, there has been no downward movement."

Centerwall concluded with some advice to the nation's doctors: "Children's exposure to television and television violence should become part of the public health agenda, along with safety seats, bicycle helmets, immunization, and good nutrition. One-time campaigns are of little value. It needs to become part of the standard package."

As for parents of small children, Centerwall advised them to immediately invest in a TV lock and to keep the key in a safe place.

And last, for those producing and marketing what these children see, Centerwall urged them to come up with a consistent violence index which would be prominently publicized along with the program; this way, parents would know ahead of time just how violent a given show was ("Television and Violence," *Journal of the American Medical Association,* June 10, 1992).

In August of 1992, a landmark event occurred: *TV Guide* itself, a magazine which is normally viewed as an apologist for the entire television industry, shocked media scholars by their cover story: "Is TV Violence Battering Our Kids?"—one of the harder-hitting such articles during the last couple of years. Featured were a number of big names in the American arena.

Neil Hickey observed that "More televised violence than at any time in the medium's history is flowing into American homes. It is coming from many more sources than ever before—from video, pay-per-view, and cable, as well as from the broadcast network and stations. The overwhelming weight of scientific opinion now holds that televised violence is indeed responsible for a percentage of the real violence in our society. What is new is that psychologists, child experts, and the medical community are just now beginning to treat televised violence as a serious public health issue—like smoking and drunk driving—about which the public needs to be educated for its own safety and well-being."

According to Hickey, during one 18-hour-period, on April 2, researchers noted on 10 channels the following: "1,846 individual acts of violence, 175 scenes in which violence resulted in one or more fatalities, 389 scenes depicting serious assaults, 352 scenes involving gunplay, 673 depictions of punching, slapping, dragging, and other physically hostile acts, 226 scenes of menacing threats with a weapon.

"Newer program forms like music videos and reality shows . . . are significantly increasing the amount of violence on our screens. And commercials for violent theatrical movies and TV series have become a major source of televised violence.

"News broadcasts, in their heightened competitive fervor, are peddling strong doses of murder, muggings, and mayhem, as ratings-getters.

"In fictional programming alone, we found more than 100 violent scenes per hour across the 10 outlets studied. Well over a third of all the violence (751 scenes) involved some sort of life-threatening assault. Cartoons were the most violent form, with 471 scenes.

"Unmeasured in our survey . . . were the many hundreds of hours of VCR watching that went on in that city, on that day—much of it devoted to theatrical films with violent content."

The study then moved on from Neil Hickey's commentary to that of other experts:

"The U.S. is the most violent 'civilized' country in the world" (Senator John Glenn).

"Just as our nation has more violent crime than any other industrialized nation, so too is our popular culture more violent than that of other countries. . . . In the media world, brutality is portrayed as ordinary and amusing" (Deborah Prothrow-Stith, Harvard School of Public Health).

"Our children are born into homes where the TV set is on seven hours a day. They start viewing as infants. Most of the stories they hear are not told by the parents, the school, the church, or neighbors. They are told by a handful of conglomerates who have something to sell. That has a powerful effect. . . . There's never been the type of expertly choreographed brutality that we have" (George Gerbner, Dean Emeritus, University of Pennsylvania).

"Beyond all else, television is a teacher. We know

that, because advertisers pay several billion dollars a year in order to get the teaching effect and to sell their products. It's such an effective teacher, and it's teaching the wrong message to young children. . . . I did a quick count of the premium cable movies listed last week in *TV Guide*. Over half of them were labeled 'violence' "— (Ronald Slaby, Senior Scientist, The Education Development Center).

"We now have cable, we have home video, we have fiber optics coming with 200 channels. When you have that kind of diversity, you're going to get some stuff that's terrible. If you let them, children will rent from the video store the worst bloody stuff that ever hit the market.

"I sometimes tell parents: suppose a complete stranger came into your home carrying two bags—one containing a lot of products for sale, and the other a lot of stories. And he said to you, 'You look tired. Why don't you just leave, and I'll talk to your kids here on the couch?' How many of us would say, 'Go right ahead'? You have to help parents understand that that box in the living room is not always a friend of the family" (Peggy Charren, President, Action for Children's Television).

Closing out 1992 is an appropriate article to conclude this cross-section of violence-related commentary: Alan Farnham's "U.S. Suburbs Are Under Siege." In it, Farnham built on what Richard Cohen said about crime changing the way we live and destroying our peace of mind. Farnham noted that, in just 20 years (1970-1990), the portion of our total gross output that we spend for personal security *doubled:* from 1.3% to 2.6%. And now, with the advent of car-jackings, people are driving through red lights rather than running the risk of having their cars car-jacked at the light. It used to be only in the cities that people lived continually in a state of fear. Now, maintained Farnham, fear is poisoning life in the suburbs as well.

And then he concluded with an observation which

may prove to be frighteningly prophetic: that this violence-related fear may very well be the instrument for terminating our democratic way of life and propelling us into a totalitarian state *(Fortune,* Dec. 28, 1992).

Is Winning Really "The Only Thing"?

Well, that's what famed Green Bay football coach Vince Lombardi always maintained—and, clearly, the American sports world appears to have accepted that observation as canonical truth. And not just being *a* winner—but being *the* winner is what counts—*that* sad truth is all too evident everywhere we look. Case in point, the Olympics. Americans are obviously—sometimes embarrassingly so—not happy with Bronze or Silver medals: many pout if their efforts garner anything less that the Gold.

Once upon a time in America, sportsmanship and fair play were considered far more important than whether or not you won.

> "When the One Great Scorer comes
>   To write against your name—
> He marks—not that you won or lost
>   But how you played the game."
> —Grantland Rice, *Alumnus Football.*

Not then were maxims such as "Nice guys finish last" and "Show me a good loser and I'll show you a loser" even in the lexicon of sports. Not then was the Eleventh Commandment of Sports, "Thou shalt not get caught." Not then was there implicit satisfaction, and even a sort of unholy glee, in the deliberate maiming—perhaps for life—of the opposing team's star player. Not then were individuals and teams implanting biological time bombs such as steroids inside them just so they could win at *any* cost.

As we have increasingly emphasized this "win at any cost" mentality, there have been some additional disturbing side-effects. The following were mentioned by Dr. Robert E. Gould, Professor of Psychiatry at New York Medical College:

"Today's most admired coaches teach their players that they must hate, to win.

"But sportsmanship and fair play were once part of the standards. Today's emphasis on winning for the camera and the national audience has made these ideals seem out of date and sissified. . . .

"It seems to me that as sports become more brutal, players and spectators both become dehumanized. If the point is winning without grace or dignity; if anything goes—cheating, bullying, deliberate injuries—and if violence is the name of the game, we will all be losers in the larger game of life."

Gould quoted Indiana psychologists Dolf Zillman and Jennings Bryan in terms of how violence increasingly

> *"There can scarcely exist a more bitter thought than the realization that we have lost by foul play what fair play would have won for us" (Stanley J. Weyman).*

takes center stage: that, more and more, in televised sports, "rough plays are more apt to be picked up by the camera and instant replays are scheduled more frequently for violent plays. In addition, announcers often follow violent incidents with approving comments like, 'now that's the way to make a half-back think twice before hitting the hole again' " ("TV Sports Teaches Violent Lessons," *Media & Values,* No. 36, Summer, 1986).

They also noted that sportscasters tend to highlight both the team and the individual players which are the most aggressive, the most violent—and the same for the evening TV news. As a real life corollary to all this, more and more winning at any cost, above *or* below the belt, is being emphasized in child and adolescent sports and games. The natural result is to eradicate all chances of utilizing sports in terms of building positive character traits. It also contributes no little to low self-esteem. Columnists Ann Landers and Abigail Van Buren have both, over the years, received considerable mail dealing with the inner scars made by "choosing up" in playground and school games. I can fully emphathize: not being naturally athletic, I would invariably be among the last to be chosen. I'd venture many would identify with me when thinking back to those terrible moments of decision, as the pool of unchosen players shrinks, and one knows he or she will be the ignominious last—or near last choice. I agree with psychologists who maintain that such cruel practices leave a lifelong legacy of needless pain and all too often so reinforce existing feelings of low esteem that many so stigmatized never do get up off the mat. Repeatedly categorized as losers—they *become* losers—and we are *all* losers because of it (Gould, *ibid.*).

Few things in this world are more fragile than a child's or a youth's self-esteem. That fact was vividly driven home to me years ago when I was teaching at Sacramento Union Academy. It was the last day of the school year and I was cleaning up my desk. A boy walked in. I cheerily asked him if he'd had a good year. He retorted, *"No!"* I more or less rhetorically asked "Why?" and he delivered a verbal uppercut that rocked me on my heels: "Because of you."

As it turned out, early in the year after lunch one day when I had asked the class a question, he had answered it. As luck would have it, it was one of those open-ended questions that could be answered in a number of ways—worse yet, some answers could be taken several ways, some hilariously funny. Well, he had the misfortune to "Murphy's Law" himself into an answer that embodied not only double—but *triple*—entendres. His classmates rolled in the aisles . . . and I with them. It really made our day.

Well, I had long forgotten the incident—but *he* hadn't. Three quarters of a year had passed and the terrible humiliation remained. Worst of all, he accused me, *"You* laughed at me!"

I have never been able to get that moment out of my mind—and it has colored all my subsequent human relationships. It is long past time, I believe, for us to reevaluate how we interact with people, especially children and adolescents.

Now, let's turn to the impact of prolonged viewing, a natural corollary to vicarious rather than real-life sports. Ellen Stark, reporting on a recent study conducted by Brigham Young University, noted that researchers discovered that "men who watched television three or more hours a day were twice as likely to be obese as those who watched for less than an hour."

Stark also called attention to another study, "Television and the Quality of Life," based on 13 years of research, which was published by Kubey and Csikizentmihalyis in 1990. Their findings were provocative indeed: "The longer a person watched the set, the more drowsy, bored, sad, lonely and hostile the viewer would become" ("Watching Television Linked to Obesity," *The Capital,* Oct. 29, 1989).

Today big league sports and the media have replaced the

Puritan work ethic as the primary motivating force—if "motivating" is even the right word!—for most Americans. As was true of the ancient Romans, ours has become the age of the vicarious. Instead of devoting time and energy to outdoor sports and exercise, we couch potato our years away watching others perform *for* us. As a natural result, we have become the most obese, flabby, and out-of-condition nation on earth.

Perhaps the popular table game "Trivial Pursuit" aptly capsulizes what we have become: majoring in minors and minoring in majors. In the Olympics of the Mind, most Americans weigh in as flyweights: mental pygmies.

One of my fondest early memories has to do with Thanksgivings at my paternal grandparents' home in the Napa Valley region of California. We always—young and old—played horseshoes during daylight and caroms, dominoes, etc., in the evening. There was no TV.

Today, everyone gathers in a dark room and watches a mind- and body-numbing seven hours of football. What kind of family memories will *these* days leave? Will it seem worthwhile to travel long distances in order to sit down in front of a box and watch the same imagery you could have seen had you never left home?

I think not.

Here too, then, is an area we parents need to address: how are we to raise our children so that they are both fair and good sports?

I submit that the inescapable answer will mandate either total elimination or severe curtailment of media sports.

CHAPTER 13

Divorce—The Ruined Eden

As I have immersed myself into the issues pertinent to this study, and occasionally emerged for air, the conviction has gradually been growing that I ought not to sign "Finis" on the manuscript without first tackling this prickly thing we rather glibly label "divorce." I guess, deep down, I have subconsciously tried to veer around it . . . but how can one ignore a huge iceberg that has sunk fleets of ships and left in its wake such a legacy of tragedy and tears? As this study has evolved, again and again, from so many directions, I have felt ship after ship I have been metaphorically traveling in shudder as the hull was ripped open, list, then go down with that awful sucking, gurgling noise that symbolizes the untimely death of dreams.

This iceberg is indeed monstrous, towering high into the sky, yet 90 percent of it is not even visible to the naked eye. Gigantic as it is, it nevertheless continues to grow in size, strength, and malevolence. Yes, this iceberg of divorce is none other than the proverbial "other woman" in the sad story of America in countdown-to-millennium. Let's utilize another metaphor to help us realize just what this force has accomplished. We might liken it to a mighty monkey wrench heaved into our midst, stripping the gears of the American juggernaut and leaving it a shuddering, clanking, steaming, whining piece of machinery. True, it continues to go through the motions; true, it still looms large against the sky—but the *power* is gone!

Divorce is sad enough when there are only two—however, that is not true either: what about the extended family and friends who have come to love the marital partner they are now forced to eject out of the front rooms of their lives? Cruelly forced by divorce to arbitrarily choose one and discard the other!

What about the lifelong scars on the psyche? the anguish, the bitterness, the welling hatred of the one left behind? the deep guilt of the one who initiated the break, which will reverberate through all the remaining years of their lives?

Really, when you come to think about it, there really *is* something mystical about marriage. Not live-ins—those are built on quicksand to begin with—but *marriage*. There is something about those vows—said before each other, family, friends, clergyman, and *God*—which add up to one of the only pieces of permanency we humans are permitted to have in our few transitory years on this planet.

Yet, so incredibly fragile is this thing called marriage! Even without the media. It begins so simply: boy

> *"The young think they can bind their passions with their vows—they do not yet know the appalling strength of human passion" (Elizabeth Goudge, The Dean's Watch).*

meets girl, boy and girl fall in love, boy and girl conclude that they are meant for each other, so boy and girl marry. Ah! But then! After the honeymoon high wanes, what then? What will keep this twosome together for half a century or more? Complicating the issue immeasurably is this reality: So complex are we humans that no one person can possibly answer or fulfill *all* our needs. And, for much of our lives, our hormones rage within us, demanding release. The Old Testament is strangely noncommittal about this aspect of our makeup: certainly the sexual prodigality of patriarchs such as Abraham and rulers such as David and Solomon introduce disturbing questions in this respect.

And the media gangs up on us, continually stoking the fires of sexuality "seven times hotter" than they were before. Come to think of it, it's a near miracle that *any* marriage involving hot-blooded creatures survives even semi-intact for half a century!

But, having said that, having admitted that, let's now return to our mythical man and woman who marry and set up housekeeping. . . . What comes next is normally a child. And the child completely changes the rules of the game. Nothing can possibly be the same after a child is conceived.

So much so that I solemnly submit that no husband and wife ought to even *consider* having a child until they are absolutely *certain* that their own love/friendship for each other is so strong that it will endure unbroken for the rest of their lives. Ideally, then, so as not to be confused by the honeymoon roller coaster, a couple should wait at least three years before deciding to have a child.

"But why do you get so worked up over the child variable?" you may ask, "for children are so *adaptable!*" Yes and no. Yes, children are adaptable. No, for no child is ever the same after divorce—*no matter how old the child or adult is when it occurs!*

It would be appropriate for me to step back in time 10 to 12 years. For five years, in Texas, I directed an adult degree program, and, more recently, I have again taught in another such program. The catalyst for arriving at experiential credit (academic credit based on knowledge and skills gained outside the traditional classroom) is the autobiography. The autobiography is the core around which chain of association variables naturally cluster. Never yet have I seen it fail—even after hundreds of life stories shared with these groups.

No matter whether it was 6 weeks, 6 months, 6 years, or 60 years ago, when the individual narrative approaches a divorce or separation milestone, the narration slows, the eyes cloud up, and the voice begins to quaver. There is something about separation that sledge-hammers an iron wedge deep, deep into the psyche, where it will remain, separating the world that was before from the world that came afterward. Not even reconciliation can remove the wedge chasm, for the fault once opened cannot again be closed. It is a virtual impossibility for the membrane has been seared for all time. I have seen individuals (men as well as women, it makes no difference), even in their 60s, 70s, or 80s, choke up over a divorce or separation that occurred a half to three quarters of a century before.

Surprisingly, in retrospect, even death is easier to recover from than is divorce . . . for death is part of the natural rhythm of our lives—divorce is not. Death represents a clean guillotine cut; divorce does not cut clear through, it only mutilates, mangles, disables, incapacitates. Worse yet, the blade itself remains there, flopping about in the psyche, continually inflicting new wounds as the pain-racked years go by. And not just to those affected by the act.

This fact was vividly brought home to me a number of years ago. A dear friend of mine had, in the floodtide of his hormonal importunings, fallen in love with his brother's wife, which resulted in two divorces in order that he might marry her. Half a century later, when this memorable conversation took place one day when we were alone, I asked him if he'd do it again if he had his life to live over. The instantaneousness of his resounding No! really surprised me for he apparently had a very special relationship with his second wife. He proceeded to enlighten me as to why.

"No, Joe, I wouldn't do it again . . . the price"—and here he choked a little—"was too high, was far too high."

When I asked him *what* price, he quickly enlightened me. It seems that by this one act—and there were at that time no children involved in the equation—he had set in motion chain reactions that clouded the rest of his life.

"Joe, I could not even correct my own children for their mistakes without them sneering at me, laughing in my face, 'You, *you,* Dad, attempt to tell *me* what to do . . . with the mess you've made of *your* life?' "

After my friend regained steadiness of voice, he confided in me that the sad tale didn't even end there: he could not even counsel with his wayward *grandchildren* without eliciting the same mocking response!

And that didn't even take into consideration the storm of criticism, alienation, and ostracism from family, friends, church, and community which raged around him for many a year after the act occurred, darkening his entire subsequent life and significantly affecting even his career objectives.

"No, Joe," he concluded, "it was far too high a price to pay."

I have never forgotten that conversation. We may gain forgiveness by our repentance, but that in itself has nothing to do with the ripples our stone causes as it disturbs the once placid waters of our lives: those ripples continue, gather force, and later circle back upon us with hurricane strength—as breakers, receding only to gather strength again out at sea and then thunder back upon our shores.

One of the saddest and most poignant open letters I have ever read was one written and published during the Christmas season by the Fort Worth *Star-Telegram* editors (referred to in my book *Christmas in My Heart,* Review and Herald, 1992). It was written by a middle-aged woman whose senior citizen retiree father had found another woman, deserted his wife, and moved in with this new attraction. The writer of the letter acknowledged that for years she had empathized with the children of divorce who somehow had to come to terms with a cracked foundation beneath them; but now, even at her age, with grown children of her own, she was in anguish. On holidays her embittered mother, nursing her wounds in a tiny apartment, had no room for her and the family, and was not even easy to be around. Her father and his new live-in and her family had little desire to have them intrude in *their* holiday activities. She mourned, *"I no longer have any home to go home to!"*

But a child . . . well, a child severed by the sword of divorce from the protected home we all need if we are to remain whole is faced with a far longer trail of tears. Years of being slung back and forth between parents like a Frisbee toy, never again having the luxury of knowing that any one place is really home. Oh yes, and a permanent insecurity complex. That's part of the lifelong price the abandonee pays and continues to pay. As one of these children—now an adult—put it: "It's not enough that you tell me today that I am appreciated, cherished, and loved. I've got to be told that *every day!* Continually. For I am so afraid it won't last!"

Years of having only one parent there for such things as birthday parties, games in which you participate, concerts in which you perform, holiday get-togethers, your own engagement and wedding, the high days in your children's lives—the ripple-effect rolls on and on and on—outlasting a battalion of Energizer batteries (of recent advertising fame).

Nothing can ever be the same again—sort of like Robert Frost's moving "Out, Out!" when a buzz saw cuts off a boy's hand:

> "The boy's first outcry was a rueful laugh,
> As he swung toward them holding up the hand,
> Half in appeal, but half as if to keep
> The life from spilling. Then the boy saw all—
> Since he was old enough to know, big boy
> Doing a man's work, though a child at heart—
> He saw all spoiled. 'Don't let him cut my hand off—
> The doctor, when he comes. Don't let him, sister!'
> So. But the hand was gone already.
> The doctor put him in the dark of ether.
> He lay and puffed his lips out with his breath.
> And then—the watcher at his pulse took fright.
> No one believed. They listened at his heart.
> Little—less—nothing!—and that ended it.
> No more to build on there. And they, since they
> Were not the one dead, turned to their affairs."

"He saw *all* spoiled"—that's what divorce does. It takes a God-blessed union of two hearts and *legally* absolves them of their mutual promises. But the price? Ah! The price! The price is everywhere we look in this pain-racked and terribly lonely America we see all around us today.

If America is ever to be America again we will have to change, to welcome God back into all our human relationships, especially marriage, and we must shunt the amoral media aside so that both marriage and the family will once again be for life— instead of the current six years!

It was not so half a century ago when television was new. Marriage was still for life, and that foundation was the rock upon which our society stood. The destruction of marriage and the home, like so many of the ills ravaging this people, can be directly credited to the media, for its battering ram has reduced to splinters most every wall or door that barred its way.

Today, the institutions of marriage and the home are under attack from every direction: in radio and MTV, cinema and videos, network television and cable, CDs and tapes, advertising in all its forms, pulp magazines and tabloid newspapers, obscene novels and gutter-level autobiographies—each erodes away part of what remains of these crucial institutions.

If marriage and the family are to survive, unquestionably there will need to take place a stiffening of our backbones. We as individuals, families, groups, and communities must dig in our heels and determine to regain all the territory we have lost due to our apathy or cowardice. Each one of us who stops running and makes a stand will make a major difference. As "Stonewall" Jackson put it, "One man with courage makes a majority."

For, as we have noted, "Till death do us part" has shrunk to but six years. Were we to continue our long and abject retreat before the armies of the media, before long marriage would be little more than a series of one-night stands, or rotational polygamy, if you please. This is our last chance—our last stand.

CHAPTER 14

So What Have Been the Results?

We have looked at many societal problems. Now let's take a look at results. Just what kind of children is all this producing?

The Changing American Home

Before the invention of television, the American home consisted of a father, a mother, and usually children. Compared with all the other societal changes in the half century of TV, none has had a more dramatic change than this. According to the latest census figures, only 26 percent of today's families fit the "traditional" description! The percentage has been eroding away at an alarming rate for decades. It was 31 percent in the 1980s, and 40 percent in the 1970s.

Another bellwether is the single-parent statistical change. There were 9.7 million single parents in 1990, 41 percent more than only 10 years earlier! Of these, almost all were women: 8.4 million, up 35 percent from 1980. In the 1970s, there was an 82 percent growth in single mothers. Between 70 to 90 percent of out-of-wedlock children will wind up on welfare, a staggering cost to society for such a shift away from traditional family values.

Michael Medved pointed out in a recent article that perception of the unwed state and reality are two totally different things: "Despite the fact that experimentation in out-of-wedlock child-rearing is temporarily trendy, the evidence is overwhelming that such arrangements are disastrous for the children involved. In 1985 a major research project by Stanford University's Center for the Study of Youth Development showed conclusively that children in single-parent families have higher arrest rates, more disciplinary problems in school and a greater tendency to smoke and run away from home than do their peers who live with both parents—*no matter what their income, race or ethnicity.*

"More recent data, gathered by *U.S. News & World Report* (June 1992) from the National Center for Children in Poverty, the American Enterprise Institute and the National Center for Criminal Justice, demonstrate some of the devastating handicaps faced by the offspring of unwed mothers. These children are more than twice as likely to repeat a grade in school (33 percent) than children living with both parents (13 percent); more than three times more likely (17 percent to 5 percent) to be suspended or expelled from school; and more than four times more likely to be assigned to a juvenile correctional facility. Amazingly enough, children raised by never-married mothers were nearly three times more likely (39 percent to 14 percent) to spend more than 10 years on welfare than children raised by divorced single mothers.

"Furthermore, despite Hollywood's emphasis on 'courageous' and well-heeled role models such as Murphy Brown, the economic status of the vast majority of unwed mothers is unequivocally appalling. Finding yourself suddenly saddled with a baby and no husband is one of the worst disasters that can befall an ordinary young woman, and often represents a trap that lasts a lifetime" (Michael Medved, "Hollywood Chic: Illegitimacy and Hypocrisy: Family Values Suffer at the Hands of Pop Idols," Washington *Post,* Oct. 4, 1992).

The impact of a mother on children has been so well documented that even to discuss it seems almost a moot question. Just to think of raising a child without a mother seems tragic. Yet in spite of that, we have all known mothers who just

"There is a lunacy in our existence. . . . We live by fantasies and fragments. We've destroyed the tribes and condemned ourselves to the solitude of cities. We scrabble for superfluous things and then do bloody battle to defend what we don't need. We peddle money and debase the currency we accumulate. We've turned away from the God of our fathers to haunt the parlors of wizards and mountebanks" (Morris West, "We Are Like Peasants," Harlequin).

walked away and left the father with the entire job.

But a far more likely scenario, given today's hard-to-stomach realities, is that the child is not likely to have a father at all. So what is the impact of life without father?

Recently, columnist William Raspberry tackled the issue of "phasing out father," calling attention to the societal loss resulting from fatherless families. He observed that the majority of "overwhelmingly fatherless 'underclass'. . . boys, denied the traditional male role of provider and defender—often denied any utility whatever—turn to increasingly antisocial behavior. Boys who have no fathers to guide them into manhood learn their manhood from the street to the peril of us all" ("Phasing Out Father," Washington *Post*, 1992).

Raspberry notes that mother and father each provide a unique type of direction: "A mother seeing her small child on a jungle gym is more likely to say 'Be careful!' while the father may say 'Can you climb to the top?'. . . The mother who asks 'Where does it hurt?' is not wrong, but neither is the father who says, 'You're okay, shake it off.' David Blankenhorn, director of the Institute for Family Values, asks us to 'pity the boy or girl who does not receive both of these types of love. Neither by itself is sufficient. But together they will make a whole and will add up to what a child needs!' This is the most basic reason for the importance of the two-parent homes. Blankenhorn warns that unless other strong male role models offer themselves, the boy is likely to define his masculinity in antisocial or criminal ways" (*ibid.*).

In another column Raspberry used as his discussional center-piece the tremendous impact "Daddy King" had on the life of his son, Martin Luther King, Jr.: "The younger King, as the writings of both men make clear, was very much his father's son: not just religiously and politically but also in terms of his self-confidence, his strength of character and purpose, and his impatience with racial discrimination. . . . I have come away with a renewed sense of how much it matters what fathers teach their sons, by precept and by personal example" ("The Awesome Influence of Fathers," Washington *Post*, June 21, 1992).

Students of our culture note that the absence of a father figure tends to distort a teenager's view of sexuality and parenthood. Many boys suffer from father-hunger. Sadly enough, many of them become fathers while still children themselves, unable psychologically or financially to cope with raising a family—with desertion therefore almost a certainty. Girls, too, suffer from father-hunger. As a result they may date older boys or men who serve as surrogate fathers to them.

TV's Role in These Changes

"Dear Ann Landers,

"Our 17-year-old daughter told us she was spending the night of the valentine ball at her girlfriend's house, but we have since learned she and two of her girlfriends spent the night with three boys at a motel. I was disappointed but not surprised.

"I have read that producers of prime-time TV have chosen to portray their teenage role models as having sex when they turn 18. One show featured a high school girl losing her virginity on prom night. No wonder one of my daughter's friends said, 'What do you think prom night is for, anyhow?'

"The message our kids get from TV is that teens feel there is something wrong with them if they haven't had sex by the time they are 18. What if the producers decide next year that sex at 16 is okay? Maybe the next year it will be 12.

"I am tired of television being a co-conspirator in lowering the code of ethics in this country."

Landers responded: "What can be seen on daytime TV is embarrassingly provocative these days, and the stuff on at night is shocking" ("Heartsick in Alabama," a 1992 column. Used by permission.).

"It's quite easy for me to think of a God of love mainly because I grew up in a family where love was central and where lovely relationships were ever present. It is quite easy for me to think of the universe as basically friendly mainly because of my up-lifting hereditary and environmental circumstances" (Martin Luther King, Jr., Autobiography, quoted in "The Awesome Influence of Fathers," Washington Post, June 21, 1992).

But what about the effects on the children?

When you put all this together and place these jaded, worldly-wise far-beyond-their-years children in a classroom, what do you get? Dorothy Cohen responded to this question by quoting a nearly burned-out teacher she had recently interviewed:

"Things are getting harder and harder in school—in my job, that is. I'm really concerned about the kids. . . . I feel that TV is very destructive. They know a lot of facts, but seem unable to put thoughts together and come up with anything from it at all. They live in a world where everything is loud and brassy. No subtleties, no awe, and they show so little emotion. It's hard to find out how they feel about things. And sometimes I think the only thing that's funny to them is when someone falls on his face. Everybody talks at about 100 decibels and nobody listens. . . . How their motors are racing! Nobody wants to do anything extra, academically. Curiosity is very rare, with exceptions, such as a second grader who said, 'I want a book with pictures of big boobies.' Another second grader had 12 photos of sexual intercourse in his pocket. Really sad to have to grow up so fast and miss the good things in childhood. First graders are asking for copies of *Jaws*. . . . Yet they're afraid when I turn out the lights to show a film" (Jerry Mander, *Four Arguments for the Elimination of Television*).

Interview With a Fourth-Grade Teacher

This book bristles with secondary source material, so having a fourth-grade teacher in our home Christmas vacation was too difficult to resist. Thus Kimberly Palmer represents my one primary source interview.

I posed a number of questions to her: What is it like to teach fourth grade today? What are the kids like? Are there differences between those who watch a lot of TV and those who do not?

She thought a while, then responded as follows. *Generally speaking*—for there are always exceptions to any rule—these are the differences she perceived:

The child who watches a lot of television (media child) tends to be less willing to follow directions or listen to counsel.

The media child is more aggressive and tends to feel that such aggression is natural and to be expected.

The media child tends to have a muddled value system and is crippled by a distorted sense of what is right and what is wrong.

The media child, even in the fourth grade, is already permissive sexually in outlook.

The media child, instead of utilizing family, church, or school role models for mentoring, emulates instead media figures—even speech, mannerisms, and behavior.

The media child dislikes reading of any kind and resists the opportunity to develop writing skills.

The media child is uncreative, lethargic, and utterly lacking in imagination.

The media child has a distorted and warped sense of reality and the world—likely to live in a state of perpetual fear.

As for children who live in a home where there is either no television permitted or strong parental control and mediation, these children, generally speaking, are eager to learn; on field trips, are much more likely to ask questions than are media children; enjoy reading; enjoy writing; are creative; and are enthusiastic about life in general.

> *"Television creates an environment that assaults and overwhelms the child; he can safely respond to it only by bringing into play his shutdown mechanisms and thus becomes more passive"* (T. Berry Brazelton, cited in Gary Turback, "Pulling the Plug on TV Addiction," Kiwanis, January 1978).

I concluded the interview by asking her what advice she'd be willing to give the readers of this book. Following are her suggestions:

"If you allow television-viewing at all, strongly control it! Be sure and put a lock on the set, for your child can be seared for life by some of the imagery being broadcast on network and cable— and it can take only seconds to do the job!

"If you do permit television-viewing, do not permit them to watch without your watching the set with them. The students who make it through the best are those whose parents continually dialogue with them about what is being viewed, how valid each commercial is, and whether it encourages unreal expectations or not; does the commercial mesh with Christian values? If not, why? The same with the programming itself. In other words, develop your child's critical thinking.

"Remember, if you eliminate TV or control it, there have to be replacements! You have to be there for them. But isn't that what parenting is all about?

"If you do let them watch TV, choose wholesome programming such as PBS and Discovery shows, *National Geographic,* etc.

"You can greatly enrich their lives by selectively showing Christian videos, as well as nature and foreign language videos.

"Talk to your children. Be there for them. Confer with them—don't take them or their concerns for granted. *Never stifle their questions!*

"Don't ever let the child call the shots but do permit the child to develop individuality and imagination. Be democratic but remain the parent.

"By all means, let the child see you and your spouse reading—a lot! Truly, we learn far more by observation than by memorization. Only if the child grows up in a home where the parents are reading role models is it at all likely that the child will develop good reading skills and a personal love for the printed word.

"Take the child on walks into nature. Make every walk, no matter how close to your home, a learning experience. Learn about the world together.

"Get a year's pass to museums, zoos, etc. You will be amazed at how the child will learn things each time, and want to repeatedly return. Go regularly to your library, and read out loud or together—but read!" (Personal interview with Kimberly Palmer, fourth-grade teacher at Redlands Jr. Academy in Riverside, California; interviewed in Arnold, Maryland, on January 1 and 2, 1993.)

Nancy Larrick, college professor and author, after considerable research, came up with 10 identifying characteristics of these children of television:

"1. They have a very short attention span.

"2. They seem to thrive on noise, strife, and confusion.

"3. They are very worldly in their outlook and attitudes (are prematurely jaded and cynical about life, and are very conversant about sex, government corruption, and adult fears before they have so much as read their first book!).

"4. They have little respect for adults (including parents and teachers), for the world they constantly watch is filled with lawbreakers, schemers, swindlers, sexual perverts, drug pushers, and low-IQ females who 'prattle' on commercials.

"5. They regard school as both irrelevant and as a punishment.

"6. They are filled with hostility or fear—and are prone to settle things with violence.

"7. They do not get enough sleep—and what they do get is of poor quality.

"8. They are prone to anti-interpersonal relationship values.

"9. They are unwilling to cooperate with others.

"10. They are anti-democratic, and prejudiced against minorities" (Nancy Larric, "Children of TV," *Teacher*, Sept. 1975).

Now, let's compare these 10 media-induced results with the qualities every child ought to develop during these years in order to be a successful person in later life. According to Marie Winn, the following are absolutely crucial:

1. The child must develop the ability to work well with people, starting with members of the family. These are the years when qualities such as patience, tolerance, generosity, selflessness, and willingness to defer gratification of desires are best learned—as is the ability to express well the emotions.

2. The child must develop the ability to make personal choices. If the child is ever to grow up into an inner-directed, as opposed to other-directed, adult, the groundwork for that will begin during these early years. This development and use of the power of choice, based on inner conviction of perceived right and wrong, is essential to any kind of successful living.

3. The child must develop basic skills for effective communication. It is during these earliest years that patterns are set for later growth: first in speaking, then in reading and writing.

4. The child must accumulate a backlog of real-life experiences in which he or she has faced a situation and handled it or failed. These sorties into the real world from the protected sanctuary of home enable the child to gain self-confidence; discover strengths and weaknesses, likes and dislikes; and gradually evolve a unique voice. If the adult is not to be a mere clone of others, the emergence of individuality must have begun very early.

5. The child must develop the ability to gather information and interpret it into useful categories—to truly understand. If the individual is ever to progress beyond mere rote parroting, to be able to conceptualize forests as well as trees, to be able to synthesize raw data and make sense out of it—in other words, to become a thinking, educated adult—it will be achieved early on, as a natural result of trial and error.

6. The child must develop and integrate his/her personally

accepted set of social and moral values. These values will gradually coalesce as a result of observation and imitation. If what the child hears is synonymous with what the child sees and experiences, the result is usually emulation. Children tend to emulate their favorite adult role models. The mentoring process begins at birth (*The Plug-in Drug*, pp. 7, 8).

As parents, it is our duty to be aware of the need for continual growth in these areas, and to be there for the child as the exploration and development occurs, assisting with positive reinforcement and example.

Let's face it: we are all creatures of procrastination—always telling ourselves that there will be time sometime, somehow, somewhere, to accomplish what we don't really relish doing today. Nowhere is this more true than in this profesison that none of us have ever trained for called "parenting." We are always so busy, and time passes at such an ever-accelerating rate that, before we realize it, our "baby" has graduated from college and is leaving home for good. Only then do many of us take stock, Monday morning quarterback, and regret decisions or actions we procrastinated on until it was too late.

One of these absolutely *crucial* early decisions has to do with physical fitness. Twenty-five years later, it will be too late to undo—*would you believe six?*

According to growth specialist, Dr. Harold Habenecht of Andrews University, "*60 to 70 percent of the child's physical growth is completed* before *entering first grade!*" ("Childhood Obesity," unpublished manuscript, Andrews University, Berrien Springs, Michigan, 1977).

What this clearly means is that this all-important stage of the individual's rocket virtually determines the lifetime physical conditioning, health, endurance, stamina! Even the muscle tissue and bone density are established during those first six years. So it ought not to be surprising that just as a child who has been active, lean, fed a healthful diet, given sufficient outdoor exercise as well as rest, will face adulthood with powerful forward momentum . . . just so the child who has been flabby, obese, inactive, and who has led a sedentary passive indoor life during those first six years, will inescapably face tremendous odds in terms of adult physical fitness, health, and a positive attitude toward life.

We have noted the above terrible price tag for procrastination: a lifetime of reduced physical fitness because the parents were asleep at the switch. But, according to Cohen and Solomon, for that same child, deprived by television from developing his or her creativity, there would be, if anything, yet a higher price to be paid: "By the age of six, one may perceive in the child at *least half* of the intellectual power, breadth, and depth that the individual will achieve later on in life"—if stunted by TV during those early years, then forever stunted intellectually will be the adult! (Akiba Cohen and Gavriel Solomon, "Children's Literate Television Viewing," *Journal of Communication,* Summer 1979).

The reason is not difficult to find: the 5,000-10,000 hours of television already assimilated dominates the child's thought patterns and more and more determines action. Studies reveal that the more TV is experienced, the more what was seen dominates non-TV hours: most subsequent conversations and play activities will reflect the media world rather than the adolescent's own outlook. In other words, the child is already in grave danger of losing eternal life, for the non-Christian media has *become* the inner-controller.

SECTION II

What We Can Do About It

CHAPTER 15

Once Upon a Time—
When We Still Had Childhood

Throughout history there have been as many types of childhood as there have been societies: some have been humane; others have been anything but! Witness the incredibly inhuman treatment of children during the Industrial Revolution (especially in Europe, but we in America were not much better). In literature, if you want to really get a feel for childhood conditions, just read Dickens—especially books like *David Copperfield* and *Oliver Twist*. Life was brutally hard for children, the day's work often starting while it was still dark and continuing until night. In the mines, children were placed in tunnels so low that a man could not get through. Often with the air poisoned by gases.

It is no wonder that so many tens of thousands of these children died before their time—such as those depicted in William Blake's sad "Chimney Sweeper." Blake's poem portrayed the brief life of the average eighteenth-century London chimney sweep. Many of them were, in effect, sold to cruel masters by their poverty-stricken parents. As young as 4 and 5 years of age, they were forced to spend all their waking hours climbing up and down inside the black soot-filled world of high chimney flues. Those who did survive to adulthood were usually diseased, stunted, or deformed. Blake begins his plea for better treatment with these plaintive lines:

> "When my mother died I was very young,
> And my father sold me while yet my tongue
> Could scarcely cry 'Weep! Weep! Weep!'
> So your chimneys I sweep and in soot I sleep."

The nineteenth century brought with it the greatest child reform movement in history, and thus, for the first time since the Renaissance, the lot of a child was an enviable one.

In America up until late nineteenth century, even in homes where children were treated well, they were not permitted to have much of a voice: "Children are to be seen and not heard" was a proverb taken literally by generations of parents. "Spare the rod and spoil the child" was another aphorism which parents took so literally that beatings were often administered sadistically. As a natural result, bonding between parent and child, or teacher and child, was most difficult.

Few Americans realize just how radical the educational and familial philosophies of educators such as Bronson Alcott were. Daughter Louisa May incorporated these modern approaches so smoothly in her books—starting with *Little Women*—that readers today fail to realize that the kindness, gentleness, absence of beatings, and resultant mother-daughter and father-daughter bonding was way ahead of its time when the book was published.

In this respect, Mark Twain's *Tom Sawyer* was a bit more in tune with the times, for Tom received his regular supply of whippings—as did his inimitable successor several generations later, Booth Tarkington's *Penrod*.

Nevertheless, conditions—with or without the ubiquitous whippings—continued to improve for children, reaching their zenith in the 1940s and 1950s, just prior to the advent of television as a factor to be dealt with in virtually every home in the nation. Consequently, I would classify the 1860-1960 time period as the golden age of childhood. Exactly in proportion to the increase in the television presence in America has been the corresponding pulverizing of childhood as we had known it during the Golden Age.

But before continuing on with what childhood has become (thanks to the media) let's step back and conceptualize both what it was and what it ought to be.

Once upon a time, before television, a parent—usually the mother—was home with the child. And this child was more than a full-time job, for she or he was filled with a sense of wonder about everything. Virtually nonstop the child would be firing questions: "Why?" "Where?" "When?"

To a child, yesterday is almost an irrelevancy, and tomorrow is so far off in the mists of the unknown that it cannot even be conceptualized. The only thing that matters to a child is today.

Usually, as we grow up, we simultaneously lose the ability to relate to what it was to be a child, to think as a child. That is why so many books or stories about children are written with such a noblesse oblige, patronizing air: unconscious verbal put-downs.

One of the few authors I have ever found who was able, as an adult, to still think and conceptualize like a child, is Elizabeth Goudge. Reading her books, you will say over and over, "She's right! That's just the way I felt as a child." Only with Goudge do I really feel I am, for the moment, a child again—consequently, I am asking her to step in now to help me with this section.

"Children . . . with the dew of heaven scarcely dry upon their wings and eyes and ears that still can see and hear, tread sweet, wild ways and have no words to tell of them. When they have learnt to pick and choose a telling word and a descriptive phrase the wings have fallen from their shoulders and the old ways are closed. Age has little left to tell of but memories and the trembling hope of returning one day to the old paths" (Elizabeth Goudge, *Island Magic*).

"Happiness is hidden in life like gold in the rock, and there are many different ways of tunneling down to it. A child's instinct will tell him which way is best for himself to tackle. Try and make him tackle the tunneling a different way and he'll run amok: lay a fuse and blow up the whole thing, himself, and the gold, and all" (*ibid.*).

Again and again Goudge reminds us that a child is the most fragile and delicate of all creatures and hence should be treated tenderly, with respect, and given room to flower in her or his own way. Above all, a child must not be programmed externally—as by the media—or the child will, in Goudge's words, "run amok." And in this respect, how appropriate this observation: "There's something within each of us—call it what you like—a core of personality—a flame—an indwelling spirit—to be true to it is to suffer a continual martyrdom of discipline and to be false to it is to burn in hell" (*ibid.*).

Were Goudge writing today, undoubtedly she would be appalled at how we are permitting the media to annihilate both the human spirit and any sense of discipline in terms of our actions.

Goudge also reminds us of how crucial the development of the imagination is for a child . . . and that it must be permitted to establish its own flow channels.

An earlier voice who spoke about children with power and empathy was the great French writer Victor Hugo.

Hugo was greatly concerned about the soul in young people,

and observed in *Les Misérables*: "There is one spectacle greater than the sea: that is the sky; there is one spectacle greater than the sky: that is the interior of the soul. . . .

"The unknown is an ocean. What is conscience? It is the compass of the unknown. Thought, meditation, prayer, these are the great mysterious directions of the needle. Let us respect them. . . .

"The soul does not give up to despair until it has exhausted all illusions."

Hugo then moves on to his deep concern for protecting the soul of a child, for ensuring that it is sheltered sufficiently so that its growth is natural and sure. And for this task he saw no one more perfectly equipped for the perilous journey—side by side with the child—than the mother.

"The soul of a young girl should not be left in obscurity; in later life, all too sudden and vivid mirages spring up, as in a camera obscura. She should be gently and discreetly enlightened, rather by the reflection of realities than by their direct harsh light. A useful and graciously severe half-light that dissipates puerile fear and prevents a fall. Nothing but the maternal instincts, a wonderful intuition combining the memories of the maiden and the experience of the woman, knows how this half-light should be applied, and of what it should be formed. Nothing can make up for this instinct. To form the mind of a young girl, all the nuns in the world are not equal to one mother."

One cannot read this idealized picture of the gradual and natural unfolding of the realities of life, in the life of a child, without shuddering as one conceptualizes what our media does to this process—what it does to the development of the soul!

What a child is, of course, is a creature in the process of becoming. We ought to—before even deciding to bring a child into the world—decide what we would do with the child. The Creator gives us no greater (or more frightening) responsibility in life than to raise a child. Not just to sire and conceive it, not just to feed and clothe it, not just to develop physically and educate it—but to so nurture the soul that the adult will love the Lord and be eager to minister to the needs of His lambs and to be in tune with God instead of Madison Avenue.

Now, *that's* a challenge!

Raising a child can be likened to teaching a class. Through many years of trial and error I have learned that, discipline-wise, one can always loosen the reins, but once in progress, one can only with great difficulty tighten up. I am a nice guy if I gradually get more humane throughout the year, but I am Simon Legree if I try to become a stricter disciplinarian as the year progresses.

The same is true with the child. Initially you watch your toddler's every step, recognizing that 30 seconds' worth of inattention can very well spell the difference between your child's life or death. Gradually, as the child develops and begins to reason and develop a sense of responsibility, the reins can and should be loosened. The process continues—and sometimes it will be discovered that too much slack was given too soon. Rarely is there a graceful way out for such a misstep—and the consequences are often tragic and lifelong. Of course, too slow a release results in an entirely different set of problems. To get it just right every time is a mighty difficult balancing act.

Eventually, there should arrive the day when your son or daughter is a child no longer, and should be set free and accepted on an entirely different basis—as a dear and cherished friend. But once the cord is cut, there should never be any kind of an attempt to reattach it. Life just doesn't work that way.

It has been said that there are two things we should give our children: "Roots—and wings."

I don't know of anyone who has articulated better than Dorothy Law Noble just what it takes to make a success of the perilous profession called parenting. She titled it,

Children Learn What They Live

"If children live with criticism,
   They learn to condemn.
If children live with hostility,
   They learn to fight.
If children live with ridicule,
   They learn to be shy.
If children live with shame,
   They learn to feel guilty.
If children live with tolerance,

They learn to be patient.
If children live with encouragement,
They learn confidence.
If children live with praise,
They learn to appreciate.
If children live with fairness,
They learn justice.
If children live with security,
They learn to have faith.
If children live with approval,
They learn to like themselves.
If children live with acceptance and friendship,
They learn to find love in the world."

CHAPTER 16

Which Direction to Go?

Which direction to go?

Now that we have articulated the magnitude of the problems facing us, it is time to search for solutions. I would guess that there is a lot of common ground we can agree on, whether we be Protestant, Catholic, Jewish, Hindu, Muslim, Buddhist, or Shinto. However it is that we perceive the Deity of the universe, we would certainly agree that we would hope that the product, each of us and our children, would embody certain qualities: would be ethical, fair, loving, caring, kind; respectful to the elderly, the children, and those unable to defend themselves; industrious, diligent, intelligent, innovative, creative, articulate; and have effective interrelating skills. These are qualities all people share, regardless of religious doctrine.

Now that we have established the premise that all of us are brothers and sisters on this planet, fellow travelers to the grave, all that remains is to arrive at solutions we can agree on.

It would seem that the question which needs to be addressed first is the one that ties most directly to the dispensation of that huge block of time equivalent to all our work on the job during our lives—that block of time which up until now we have dedicated to watching television.

Shall we continue watching it or not?

Shall we let our children watch it? our teenagers?

If we do, what guidelines shall we institute?

If we do not permit them to watch it, what are we going to do with this treasure chest of time that will suddenly appear in our vault?

Pulling the Plug

It is possible that, after you review the material in this study, you may decide to throw out the television set altogether. There is plenty of precedence for this sort of thing.

In Missoula, Montana, Bill and Diana Smith put the TV set in the closet . . . and waited for the explosion—that never came. Instead, the kids played together, stayed outside more, became involved with a new puppy and kittens, watched the tiny creek overflow, read books. The cable TV money went for children's magazines and games. Stories were read at bedtime; Saturday morning became a family affair. They went fishing together, took up square dancing —and there are no regrets.

Victor Cline, Utah psychologist and media expert, and his wife pulled the plug. The children's complaints ceased one week later. The kids went

"Nothing in life . . . is so lovely as a fresh beginning, and nothing breeds more courage. One can imagine the fresh beginnings of our lives burning like prophetic torches along the way, crying aloud the good news in the character of flame upon darkness. . . . Sorrow and joy are always twined together in life. . . . Every fresh beginning is a new birth and must have its pain as well as its joy, and without these fresh beginnings, there would be no life, without them we should turn sour like stagnant water in a pond. And always . . . the joy of a fresh beginning lures us on, outweighing the pain, dancing before us like a flame, so that hurrying to catch it the life in us keeps fresh and clear as a running stream" (Elizabeth Goudge, Towers in the Mist).

outside and played together more, a lot more good books were read, the homework was done on time, the chores got done, and everyone played together harmoniously.

"I finally faced the fact that television is not reformable, that it must be gotten rid of totally if our society is to return to something like sane and democratic functioning" (Jerry Mander).

Those who pull the plug quickly discover how much dissension TV watching brings into the home and how quickly it dissipates once the plug is pulled.

In a research study in a New York school, students discovered life to be meaningful—even fun—without TV. Some youngsters discovered such little known, even unknown, pleasures such as holding a conversation and reading. They helped their mothers more and did more homework. There was less family tension, and mealtimes were more pleasant.

To find out what would happen if Detroit-area families actually turned off the set for a month, the Detroit *Free Press* editors persuaded five families to find out for them.

Bruce and Lu Bertha Callaway and their two children really experienced withdrawal traumas. Lu Bertha almost went crazy without her daily soaps, and it didn't help when she phoned her mother for details and heard, "Oh, you should see it! Ron just kidnapped Karen, and Chris and Snapper are frantic." Headaches followed. The kids screamed at each other. Bruce, complaining of nothing to do at night, went from one pack of cigarettes a day to two and a half. On the other hand, before the month was over, the Callaways were actually talking with each other and the children playing more with each other, as well as spending more time with their parents. And as a serendipity, Bruce and Lu Bertha's sex life improved dramatically.

Another of the families, Ed and Rosemary Rychlewski and their eight children, reacted differently. Five days into the month Ed and Rosemary weren't talking to each other at all. However, the children read more, played dominoes and cards with their parents, and—their imaginations freed from TV—built a make-believe city in the basement. Ed, who deeply resented missing televised football, used the freed time to read newspapers, and in

"The following hour of blank screen is being brought to you by the Home Counseling Service to give members of your family a time to become reacquainted with each other."

the process blossomed into the best-informed man in his company. Not only that, but the kids started paying more attention to their homework, and Ed and Rosemary had time to help them. Everyone went to bed earlier.

Carol and Ed Shorts watched TV the least often. Nevertheless, Carol really missed her PBS programs, Ed his sports, and Vicki, 2, would walk over to the set, slap it, and cry, "Broke! . . . Fix!" Carol admitted how surprised she was to discover her dependency on television. However, Vicki was delighted when her father suddenly found time to play with her and take her for walks in the garden. Carol and Ed found themselves talking more with each other, and reading more, and Carol declared that their sex life improved by 50 percent.

Judy Mann told of her getting rid of the TV habit . . . just by taking forever to fix it. Much later, she noted: "When you get away from the television for a while and then you turn it back on, you realize how stupid the sitcoms are. The noise level of the people's conversations alone is offensive. The stories, dialogue, characters, and sets are drearily predictable. The only thing that seems to change from season to season is the commercials. It is a terrible time-waster" ("Turning Off the TV Habit," *Washington Post*, Apr. 20, 1990).

Mann concluded her column by calling attention to television's contributions to increased violence, obesity, sexual promiscuity, alcohol consumption, poor physical fitness, poor scholarship, passivity, etc. And her coda: "Television is a lot like smoking. You only realize what a rotten habit it is once you've stopped."

Coleman McCarthy, recounting his experience, observed that instead of rushing through the evening meal, his family of five actually ate peacefully and leisurely. Now the family stays at the playground until the children are ready to leave. Now he and his wife actually have time to talk to each other. They had been afraid that there would be a problem in terms of the kids sneaking to neighbors' houses to watch TV there—but it hasn't happened.

McCarthy suggests that the following announcement be beamed into every one of the homes in America that have TV sets:

"Ladies and gentlemen, until further notice we are ceasing our broadcasts. The programs we had planned are now seen to be dull, banal, pointless, not worth your time and not ours. Don't turn to another channel, because you'll only be insulted there too—insulted by the programs and by the corporate advertisers who want to gull you into buying products you can live well, even better, without.

> *"All of us had become adjusted to living with a stranger in the house. Is there any more basic definition of a television than that? . . . I was not only paying personally for the stranger-salesman in my house, but he was often manipulating or lying to my children. . . . If the televisers want to teach my children something, I suggest subjects such as obedience to parents, sharing toys with brothers or sisters, kindness to animals, respect for grandparents"* (Coleman McCarthy, *"My Turn: Ousting the Stranger From the House,"* Newsweek, Mar. 25, 1974).

"Come forward and turn off your set. When the die-out dot appears, get up and take a walk to the library, and get a book. Or turn to your spouse and surprise [him/her] with a conversation. Or call a neighbor you haven't spoken with in months. Write a letter to a friend who has lost track of you. . . . Meanwhile, you'll be missing almost nothing" (Coleman McCarthy, "My Turn: Ousting the Stranger From the House," *Newsweek*, Mar. 25, 1974).

If there were simple answers that really worked, life would be ever so much easier. But there aren't. Life is almost unbelievably complex. And the dangers of overreacting are as great as the problem itself. How difficult it is for us humans to hold to a centrist position, tilting to neither extreme! We have learned in this book the grave dangers inherent in contemporary mass culture, but there are equally grave dangers in swinging to the other extreme, isolating ourselves in pockets of pseudovirtue so that we can hide away from temptations and from those who are not as "good" as we are. No such utopian or monastic experiment has ever worked well over a long period of time.

On the other hand, so frightening is today's cultural alternative that unless we consciously and consistently stick to a Christ-centered position and direction, our success odds are most dim.

Also complicating our decision is how unbelievably complex our lives are. Case in point is the age factor: What is right or acceptable for one stage in one's development is likely to be totally wrong for another—hence the difficulty in raising children representing a wide age spread in the same house. An 18-year-old cannot be treated as an 8-year-old or a 3-year-old. Frankly, I don't know that even Solomon had the answer for that! The best I can do is to approach one age level at a time.

Early Childhood

It has taken me a long, long time to reach my current position. For most of my life I have advocated a centrist position here, unless the parent lacked the guts to really control the television. Today I am increasingly convicted that my earlier position was untenable. In fact, I am now convinced that before one introduces a new soul into this deeply troubled planet, husband and wife need to discuss seriously whether or not they are prepared to make some serious personal sacrifices for the long-term good of the child.

Especially crucial are the first six years, that incredibly frightening period of parental responsibility during which the child will learn half of what will be learned in the entire lifetime, during which time the physical conditioning and bone structure will be set for life, and during which time the ethical and spiritual shafts must be driven deep into the psyche, even into the soul itself, if the child is to live a truly successful life.

I no longer believe it probable that this can be accomplished very effectively with the media permitted to intrude, to represent a voice other than the parental and the spiritual. To do so inevitably blurs the focus and softens the bone structure of character. There are just too many quagmires to deal with. It would be far better for children to develop during this period their *own* reading, conceptual, and imaginational powers than to have the prefab imagery of TV blasted into the young minds.

Unless children fall in love with reading during this early period, that romance is statistically unlikely ever to occur. Abstract print is just too plain to compete on equal terms with her gorgeous sister celluloid—even adults find *that* hard.

In my own married life, my wife and I reached our moment of decision years ago when our son Greg was about 3. He had begun crying uncontrollably when she left for work, and stuttering more and more. We took stock of our meager options and concluded that her being home for our child was more important to us than were the extras her paycheck would bring in. For almost 20 years she did custom sewing, taught piano, and did court reporter steno-note transcribing in order to be home for Greg and later our daughter Michelle. As a result, the bonding between both children and their mother has been very strong. In looking back, and noting with pride what our children have become, we feel that the sacrifice was more than worth it and recommend that others do likewise. It *can* be done.

But . . . if I were to do it all over today, I would be less of a male chauvinist and assume more of the responsibility myself, adjusting my workday schedule so as to free my wife more, permit her more opportunities for escaping the claustrophobic four walls closing in on her. Today, if it is to work, husband and wife must approach that entire 20- to 25-year-period of child rearing as a *team effort*.

The Second Six Years

When Christ was only 12 He confounded the chief theologians of His culture. Obviously His parents had spent thousands of hours with Him, answering His questions and counteracting the unwholesome town environment of Nazareth ("Can there any good thing come out of Nazareth?") Second only to the first six years of one's life is the second.

During this period comes the intrusion of a new force into the child's life: the school. With the advent of teacher, the parent is no longer perceived to be supreme. Powerful new teacher- and peer-related influences come into play. It is absolutely imperative that parents know to whom they are entrusting the tender young souls of their children during this critical period of growth—and, even knowing that, monitor on a daily basis what the child is experiencing and being exposed to.

Up until very recently I was content to advise parents to begin permitting children to watch television, on a selective basis, during the second six years. But now, after studying some disturbing new data, which I have already shared, I am changing my position. I now advise—*strongly: no television at all for the first 10 years*. This includes computer or video games played on a television screen, such as Nintendo. The reason is that these games tend to become an obsession, cause hyperactivity, and greatly detract from the child's growth physically and intellectually.

Why have I made such a change in position? Well, here are several key reasons:

If you can raise a 12-year-old who is a voracious reader, is innovative, is imaginative, has a good sense of humor, has high ethical standards, loves the arts, loves the outdoors, is physically fit, loves animals, is kind, is respectful, is conscientious, cares deeply about his/her relationship with God, then you may be deeply grateful! (Joe L. Wheeler).

1. I am convinced, beyond a shadow of a doubt, that unless the child falls in love with reading *early*, develops that crucial skill well, and begins to write about what is read and experienced, there will be trouble ahead. All too clearly, once TV has been introduced, reading is likely to be quickly given a backseat. I have seen this happen again and again; and students in my college classes tell me that their cessation of reading began at the moment when TV became a key viewing factor at home.

2. I suggest that you reread Louisa May Alcott's *Little Women;* this time, pay particular attention to the creativity expressed by the March sisters (in real life, patterned closely on the

Alcott sisters); note how they were avid readers and writers—even writing and producing their own plays. It is difficult to visualize a family of the TV generation exercising that degree of creative articulation—what we are producing are lazy, out of condition, couch potatoes who are capable of little more than reflecting, in a haphazard way, what they have been exposed to. They are creatively deprived, cursed with idea-poor blood.

3. Up until the double-digit years, as we have already learned, the child is still unable to differentiate between reality and unreality on the screen, cause in itself not to prematurely introduce the television set as a family member.

4. Once TV has been introduced, studies conclusively prove that creative and intellectual growth are likely to take a nosedive—at *whatever* age heavy viewing occurs—studies have shown that even senior citizens lose their intelligence as a result of heavy viewing!

I have two recommendations to be weighed (one against the other) on the child's 11th birthday:

1. Continue the total TV blackout for two more years, or

2. Permit extremely limited and controlled viewing to take place.

If there are smaller children in the family, I would unhesitatingly opt for the former. At any rate, even without smaller children, in choosing the latter I would do so regretfully, because the losses would undoubtedly outnumber the gains.

The first 12 years are so crucial in terms of a person's life and potential, both on this earth and in the hereafter, that we (parents, would-be parents, family, educators, friends, and support system) need to approach them a lot more seriously than we ever have before.

Three generations ago, parents just didn't have to be effective parents in order to do a half adequate job of raising a child. In those days, there was an extended multigenerational family which remained an integral part of the growing-up process. True, it was already changing: with the urbanization of America also came the disintegration of the extended family. This is a tragic loss for a number of reasons.

The child is the greatest loser of all for it is an inescapable fact of life that young marrieds are run ragged by their multitudinous involvements: akin to a juggler keeping half a dozen oranges in the air at once. Thus, the parents are not able to spend as much time with their children as all might wish. On the other hand, Grandpa and Grandma are finally getting through life's worst hurdles so that they can begin to enjoy life—thus, the opportunity to be with grandchildren seems very desirable to them. And great grandparents, if still alive, will have even more time to spend with these new descendants.

The older generations have the potential to be the deciding factor in terms of which direction the child will go. They are the ones who pass on family history, family traditions, and family values. Because of the age difference and because they aren't saddled with the children for life, the grandparents are more likely than parents to become cherished friends with this next generation. Once this deep bond is established, if retained, it can represent a crucial behavioral keel during the stormy teenage years. In fact, as the child is cutting the parental umbilical—which is natural and to be expected—it may be providential the relationship with the grandparents remains a constant.

And in one-parent homes, grandparents may well represent survival itself! And their influence magnified many times. Sociologists and anthropologists have long known that in societies where the aged are highly respected and honored, those societies are usually happy above the average; furthermore, juvenile delinquency is usually low, for to behave reprehensibly brings dishonor on the entire family.

In American history, there is a direct correlation between the breaking up of the extended family and the disintegration of the family structure itself. In the days when the three generations wandered at will in and out of each other's homes, and always celebrated religious, patriotic, and family high days together, there was a familial strength that helped to hold together both marriages and families.

It is also important that parents continue this interaction with their parents, but on a new plane—as friend to friend rather than as child to authority figure. Hopefully, this new relationship will result in a very special kind of adult bonding. It will be needed, for there will most likely be tough years ahead. Today, we are told that the average woman is, statistically, likely to spend more years of her life caring for an aging parent than she is for any of her children. Again, ample reason to keep all three generations interacting with each other.

And as for the senior members of the family, not to be needed, or wanted, at the very time when retirement makes family ties doubly important, is tantamount to death itself. And when one's dreams are gone, one's goals are met, and no one seemingly cares whether or not you live or die—well, you die.

How tragic it is to walk into most any rest home in America—their stench is a constant. There has to be a way to counteract that! You walk down the hall and look at people who are chronologically still comparatively young but who have given up on life because people—especially family—have given up on them. "No one visits him, visits her" is true of all too many. And that becomes a vicious cycle, for life has a way of coming full circle: as you do unto others, sooner or later is done back to you. As you treat your parents, just so, your children will do unto you.

It is long past time for us as a society to seriously begin to seek ways to bring our extended families back together again.

These first 12 years can be incredibly precious and happy ones if we will but make them so. Even with the intrusion of school, if parents are there enough for their children and involve themselves enough with their children during evenings, weekends, and vacations, then by the time the children reach the teen years, the bonding, trust, and friendship will be strong enough to enhance significantly, bringing the children safely into the calmer waters of young adulthood—not calm, just calmer.

Things Families Can Do Together
With the Time That Pulling the Plug Provides

1. Read together, each with his or her own book. Read out loud to the family. Take the family to a library. Build a family library. Help each child to build his or her own library. Giving inscribed books on special occasions will help in this respect. Also subscribe to newspapers and magazines.

2. Have dinner-table discussions on the order of those conducted by Leo Buscaglia's father ("My Father's Dinner Table University"). In a *Reader's Digest* article Buscaglia told how his father made every dinner an educational event, expecting each child to report to him about something new that had not been known the previous day. This way each child looked eagerly at the surrounding world, listened intently to school lessons, and generally kept the sense of wonder fairly well intact. Electric family discussions followed these

questions and answers, with frequent expeditionary side trips to the encyclo-pedia and other sources required.

3. Listen to great music together on the stereo system. Attend concerts. Encourage each child to develop at least one musical skill (instrument, voice, etc.).

4. Visit art galleries together, instructing your children about the artists, the time periods. Provide the family with books and videos about art and artists. Encourage each member of the family to take art lessons.

5. Encourage each member of the family to acquire hobbies and to develop hobby-related skills. Have hobby nights in which the hobbies can be discussed and displayed. Attend events and visit places that tie in to these hobbies.

6. Make the study of nature and God's wonderful world one of your highest priorities. Grow a garden and allocate a specific part of the garden to each child. Take frequent walks in the outdoors. On weekends take family expeditions to beauty spots—parks, lakes, rivers, mountains, seacoasts, etc. And on vacations travel to more distant places.

7. Incorporate into family life service to those less fortunate. Visit the ill, the bereaved, and the elderly, and assist them when possible. Participate in community and mission outreach programs. Encourage sacrifice in order to help others.

8. Make holidays special. Incorporate holiday-related activities and places to visit. Tie in stories and special films that best depict the true significance of the holidays.

9. Incorporate the extended family—grandparents, cousins, uncles—into the flow of family life. Tie in special occasions (family high days such as birthdays, holidays, school achievement, music or art or sport or skill achievement, religious events, etc.) to the gathering together of the extended family. Make the meals, games, music, etc., all so enjoyable that they will never want to see such traditions come to an end.

10. Learn languages. Encourage them to learn them at the earliest possible age, because the earlier they are attempted, the faster they are learned and the better the accent. There is no valid reason the entire family could not learn languages together by reading, listening to recordings, music, language videos, etc. And then, if you can, tie in visits to places where these languages are actually spoken.

11. Have frequent game nights, because few activities draw a family together more effectively than games. Especially it is a good idea to incorpo-rate games that actually teach or enhance skills. Nothing we have ever found comes even close to Anagrams as a vocabulary builder. Jeopardy is an excellent general knowledge builder.

12. Incorporate geography into family activities. Subscribe to magazines such as *National Geographic*, *Smithsonian*, and travel magazines. Encourage a friendly rivalry in terms of who can find specific countries, cities, rivers, lakes, oceans, regions, continents, etc., the quickest on maps. Offer each child incentives for learning all the key geographic places on the map: first the U.S., second the Americas, and then the rest of the world.

13. Utilize the same sort of game playing and incentives in honing their science-related and mathematical skills.

14. Participate in sewing, embroidering, crocheting, quilting, etc., with family. Men as well as women are today getting involved in these areas. Quilts offer a wonderful way to tie all the generations of a family into a creative effort as well as helping develop a real sense of family.

15. Outdoor games and sports such as horseshoes, shuffleboard, badminton, volleyball, baseball, football, basketball, tennis, swimming, hiking, skiing, etc., are another excellent way to develop the physical skills.

16. Involve each member of the family in cooking and baking. After all, today many of the most famous chefs are men, and soon enough both sexes of your family will need culinary skills.

17. Make the home comfortable so that it feels like a home rather than a motel. But it should also be a place of great beauty. Americans today are sadly lacking in the aesthetics. Surround children with tasteful art, originals where possible: oil, watercolor, photography, limited-edition prints, cels, ceramics, sculpture, etc. All teach them to value the beauty of the world.

18. Keep the home serene, with silence in which to dream. The music should contribute to this serenity. Candles or kerosene lanterns, a fire in the fireplace—each slows down the hectic pace of life and encourages reflection.

19. Especially incorporate the grandparents into the flow of family life.

20. However, with all the artistic beauty, the creations of each child, however crude, ought to be accorded a special place, thus building self-confidence and a sense of being a part of the house itself.

21. Make their friends always welcome as long as they are willing to abide by your rules and fit into your moods and activities. Many of your children's friends will be inwardly starving for a Christian TV-less home in which love and caring are ever present.

22. Teach them to be good stewards, to handle money wisely. By giving each child responsibility and paying for chores, etc., you can provide the children with money of their own to spend for odds and ends, gifts, hobbies, articles of clothing, and church-related activities such as offerings, tithe, etc.

23. Have pets if at all possible. Caring for them teaches children responsibility. Cuddling and stroking them teaches love, tenderness, and kindness. Fish in a tank enhance serenity and slow the house's pace.

24. Meals, especially evening and weekend meals, should be special, somewhat leisurely, and a high point of those days.

25. Family council meetings are an excellent method of achieving esprit de corps and counteracting the tendency we parents have to pontificate.

26. Encourage children to keep up a correspondence with friends and relatives, especially absentee siblings or grandparents.

27. Encourage children always to express gratitude quickly. Children are not naturally grateful. It is a skill that must be taught. A parent can help encourage that skill by writing thank-you notes to the child for gifts the child gave or for special achievements. Whenever a relative or friend gives the child something, insist on a prompt written (telephoned is not enough) response.

28. Where absentee family or extended family exist, be sure to develop a

family tradition of phoning—usually at the same time—each week. By so doing, you also increase the likelihood that your children will remain in contact with you when they become adults, for habit patterns, both good and bad, are mighty hard to break.

29. Also each member of the family, from the oldest to the youngest, should participate in the many chores it takes to keep a home running smoothly and in an attractive condition. Especially is this essential with working parents. But it is also very important for the child's sake. If children fail to carry their own weight, fail to give as well as receive, they will grow up feeling that the world owes them a living. Children do not develop well when raised by martyr parents who deprive themselves of everything in order that the children may hog it all!

30. Take time for God and for values. Few of us pause any longer for daily devotionals, and we are all paying the price. The truth of the matter is that relationships—be they husband and wife or parent and child—rarely survive long without the cementing factor of a Higher Power. And God is just, whom few of us make time for today.

Third Six Years

By the thirteenth year it will be time to begin introducing your son or daughter to the media, for if you do not do so, the results can be tragic, veering into self-righteous fanaticism or media excess. One is as bad as the other.

Obviously your teenager will have had some interaction (at school, parties, programs, etc.) with television, and most likely you will occasionally have used your VCR when you found something special you wanted to show the whole family. But now you commence to teach your teenager how to differentiate between what is good and of value and what is not good and a waste of time. It will be very important that you release the reins slowly.

Initially, with your teenager, you will most likely continue your policy of no TV on school nights—with only occasional, agreed-upon exceptions. And be extra careful during vacations, as that is where or when many bad habits begin that later prove very difficult to break.

You will also wish to build during these years on the skills and interests acquired earlier. Now is the time to assist in developing these gifts so that the children become really proficient in at least one area. Continue language study, for every year that passes makes acquiring a natural accent or pronunciation that much more difficult.

The name of the game now is "ever more choices." Not even

now should unlimited media access be granted, for adolescents are still not prepared to handle the volatile choices that bodily changes are flinging at them. These are likely to be the roughest years of all, because of peer and media pressure to try all kinds of substance abuse, to accept sex outside of marriage as a natural lifestyle, to regard homosexuality or lesbianism as an acceptable way of life, to push God and the church aside as being irrelevant to contemporary society, to put down parents and their values as being archaic and naive, etc. But together—with father, mother, child, extended family, and God—even these years may be bridged successfully.

It is clearly not enough to protect the soul of the child alone. That protection should continue through the adolescent and teen years, gradually permitting more and more choices while still retaining a parental presence. Here is yet another arena we parents have surrendered to the enemy by default. How well I remember a discussion I had a few years ago with the founder and director of Kids of Bergen County (in New Jersey). Like many Christian parents, he and his wife mistakenly assumed that no child of theirs would ever have a drug problem. Well, they were proved wrong . . . and out of it grew this program that has helped parents be parents. He observed that so many parents seem afraid of being parents— what if their teenager doesn't like it? To that he retorted, "Don't worry. You'll be friends again when your son is 28. And he'll bless you for your having been a parent and not a buddy." The truth of the matter is that many a teen is crying out for the parents to assume that adult role.

The Fourth Six Years

There's not much left you can do now except ring true to all that you have been teaching and evidencing by your example. The time has come to make a seismic change in the relationship: from being a parent to being a friend; from providing a great deal of slack in the relationship to releasing altogether. If you have done your job well, the results will warrant all you gave up in the interest of your child's eternal well-being.

The Young Adult Years

Married, With Children—These represent perhaps the most

frantically-paced years of our lives. It seems like everything happens at once. With college over, you marry and both of you start careers; children come along; you keep taking classwork in order to stay current with your profession; you work at keeping marriage intact; you operate a taxi service, now shuttling your own children here, there, and everywhere; you faithfully meet their teachers at parent-teacher conferences and attend every last program your little darlings are in; you participate in church and community organizations; and the list goes on and on.

Occasionally during these whirlwind years you will pause briefly for a breath and ask yourself if you are really accomplishing anything significant. The reality that you don't see during these years of blurred motion is that, in your parenting roles, you are accomplishing—or not accomplishing—the single greatest work of your lifetime: raising children to be loving, caring, and Christian, while wrestling all the while, like Jacob, with an amoral world that fiercely fights for possession of your own flesh and blood.

Unmarried, or Married, Without Children—The young adult unmarried years can be incredibly productive ones, for one can plough the ocean of energy it takes to raise a child into other human relationships and in creativity. One of the tragedies of our time is that so few really use their hours away from the job wisely.

It is so easy to come home from work and, with a sigh of relief that the paycheck part of the day is over, flop down into the favorite easy chair, push the remote, and check out the TV. Well, one program leads to another, one promo leads to another, and before you know it another evening is gone forever—with nothing to show for it. Nay, worse than that: with a loss of high ground, a loss of productivity, a loss of creativity. There will now be additional hours of prefab imagery competing in your creativity chamber with the original ideas that still remain. And each time you repeat this scenario, you displace more, leaving you with less and less articulating power.

But if you do harness the extra creative energy and time the unmarried state permits you to devote to the nonfamilial, there is no valid reason at all that you should not churn out a continual flow of achievements. Mozart pulled it off even while being married, but it was much more difficult.

Adults in Mid-passage

Now, at last, with the children grown, the time has come to devote time to your own journey. Here is where so many of us fail: We fail to realize that we are *always becoming*. We are ever changing from something we have been to something higher or something baser. Nature abhors long plateaus. Now it is that we will need to reread the passage from C. S. Lewis's *Mere Christianity* that deals with the little marks on the soul.

If there is any period of religious life that we adults have failed to take seriously, it is this one. We have mistakenly assumed that once we had crested Fool's Hill and become adults, we were home free . . . that we could read or see anything without it affecting us. Belatedly we are discovering just how major a fallacy this assumption really is. We have learned that only death releases us from being changed for good or evil in this life.

Senior Citizen Years

Even as senior citizens we have the potential to destroy ourselves and those dear to us by wrong choices. It means that watching even the standard fare of what popular literature and the media has to offer has, built-in, the seeds of our disintegration, the cracking of our moral and ethical selves . . . whatever our chronological age.

And All of Us Together

Not often does a media scholar evaluate television in terms of what it does to not just preschoolers or children, but all ages. However, George Comstock of Columbia University did just that. As the result of considerable research, he arrived at what he considered eight major changes for the worse as a result of Americans' love affair with the tube. (See his book *Television and Human Behavior*.)

1. *Sleep*—Instead of sleeping well, the individual remains almost continually in a stage of "vague fatigue."

2. *Social Gatherings*—Personal relationships with relatives and friends have been significantly reduced—as is involvement in community life and service.

3. *Reading*—It has been greatly reduced because TV shunts even newspapers aside, brooking no rivals in its single-minded obsession for total mind dominance.

4. *Physical Movement*—Of television Comstock observed, "There is indeed no other experience in life that permits so much intake while demanding so little outflow" (*ibid.*).

5. *Family Relationships*—Proportionally equal to the TV-watching time is the commensurate abdication of parental involvement and guidance of the child.

6. *Outdoor Activities*—Not only do TV viewers exercise significantly less; they venture outside into the sunshine and fresh air much less as well.

7. *Religious Activities*—In a major study *Time* magazine reported that TV has caused a drastic reduction in church attendance and involvement.

8. *Household Activities*—As a result of TV, less cooking is done, and there is instead an increased reliance on junk foods and high-calorie foods that are low in nutritional value.

The 23rd Channel

The TV set is my shepherd. My spiritual
growth shall want. It maketh me to sit down
and do nothing for the cause of Christ,
because it demandeth all my spare time.

It keepeth me from doing my duty because it
presenteth so many good shows I cannot miss.
It restoreth my knowledge of the world, and
keepeth me from the study of God's Word.

It leadeth me from paths of worship and service
for the sake of entertainment. Yea, though I live
to be a hundred, I shall keep on viewing my TV
as long as it shall work, for my set is my
closest companion.

Its sound and its picture, they comfort me.
It prepareth diversion for me in the face of

my responsibilities. It filleth my head with fantasy, and my imagination runneth over. Surely no good will I do in the Kingdom all the days of my life and I will dwell with my one-eyed idiot box forever.

Author Unknown

CHAPTER 17

The Apostle Paul, Saint Francis, *RoboCop*, and *Home Alone*

A few weeks ago my wife and I rented and watched the *Home Alone* video. Since it was touted as a great family film and since it had received so much play in the media, I had been looking forward for some time to viewing it.

It is a very disturbing film. It is also a key film in terms of this study, because it reveals to us how much we have changed.

In brief, for those few who may not have already seen it, *Home Alone* portrays a family getting ready for a Christmas trip to France. The setting: a mid-sized town a few hours out of Chicago. An extended family are getting ready to leave, and although it is the season of the Christ child, the mood is anything but Christian: the words, the actions, the way each person treats each other—everything is ugly. What struck me, for the first time, was this: Here, in living color, is just how far we have come from *A Wonderful Life* and *Miracle on 34th Street*. Here is Christmas divorced from Christian values. True, *Miracle on 34th Street* didn't purport to be about Christ at all, nevertheless the values represented meshed with those of Christianity.

In *Home Alone* there is a big scene, and a small boy is sent to bed without his supper. The next morning, in the hurry, he is inadvertently left behind. Two robbers are waiting in the wings to move in and clean out the house. The rest of the movie has to do with what happens when robbers meet boy. The boy, being a video kid, conducts a brilliant military campaign, almost defeating the two Abbott and Costello-type robbers, reminiscent of the endearing cartoon robber "Butch" of the 1950s. But the child conducts his warfare mostly below the belt, in sadistic delight. Almost every device he uses is designed to torture, maim, or mutilate.

There is a contrived walking into a church where he finally sees a Boris Karlov of a neighbor for the lonely old man he really is and results in "Boris's" saving him from the long-pent-up-ready-to-explode fury of the robbers once they finally catch him and have him wriggling on the wall. Obviously he is about to receive a dose of his own medicine. And the little boy helps to reconcile "Boris" and his son. But nothing rings true—especially the boy's miraculous conversion from insolent brat to loving son in the last scene.

There is precious little love shown in the movie. Even at the end, when the blitzkrieg that the threesome unleased on the house (reminiscent of Graham Greene's *The Destructors*) is somehow magically undone, the restoration of a secular family to each other—with various ones feebly attempting to don ill-fitting Christian jackets—just doesn't work! They are all hollow because none of them have within them the genuine caring love that is a natural outgrowth of a personal relationship with Christ.

Of course, *RoboCop* takes us far beyond the petty warfare of *Home Alone*. Its children are used as agents of every kind of lethal sadism and perversion modern weaponry is capable of. And these cold-blooded little killers are totally devoid of innocence, of caring, of Christian love.

Together the two films represent a wrenching revelation of just how far we have gone in destroying the very fiber of this nation—this nation that still pretends it is Christian but whose media proof texts screech out denial.

Now let me shift gears and come at the problem from a different direction. Last year in my world literature class we read and discussed Victor Hugo's *Les Misérables*. I have asked many previous classes to read the book, but it had never before elicited the response of last year's class: "Dr. Wheeler, what naive innocents Cosette and Marius are! . . . Sitting there on a park bench day after day, just talking and looking at each other!" And for the first time it really came home to me what the media had done to our conception of love—in this case, romantic love.

There is no magic to love anymore. No hauntingly beautiful, gradual unfolding of the petals of love, leading up to the ultimate full flowering of marriage and a lifetime together. No, in today's fiction and celluloid portrayals, there are no courtships. There are in today's music and MTV, in today's advertising, not even any preliminaries! Boy meets girl, man meets woman, and bam! If the chemistry is right—and it apparently almost always is—before the relationship is more than minutes old, before they so much as date a while in order to see whether or not they even *like* each other, before they so much as hold hands, before they so much as experience the rapture of that first gentle kiss . . . before any of this, within minutes they are nude and in bed with each other! This is what my students were really responding to in their response to the courtship of Marius and Cosette.

In a society without sexual preliminaries, there can be no romance! In a society without romance, there can be few illusions. And without illusions, reality overwhelms us. Media writers and producers have failed to realize that marriage, family, and lifetime commitment are the logical and God-ordained corollaries to friendship blossoming into romance and concluding with sexual intimacy. To start with that ultimate invasion of inner privacy, the sexual act, before they have had the opportunity to decide whether or not they are compatible in all the many other ways necessary to a lifetime relationship, is a travesty—an insult. And we parents have done the ultimate Pilate act: washing our hands in a moral basin, inanely declaring that we really can't do anything about what the media are doing to our children—after all, we didn't write the books or the scripts.

The time has come—indeed, is long past—when we as a Christian society need to construct stronger walls around our children, walls strong enough to protect that now-defiled sanctuary that we used to call childhood. And once we have reestablished

> *"The sweetest lives are those to duty wed,*
> *Whose deeds both great and small*
> *Are close-knit strands of an unbroken thread,*
> *Where love ennobles all.*
> *The world may sound no trumpets, ring no bells,*
> *The Book of Life the slurring record tells.*
>
> *Thy love shall chant its own beatitudes,*
> *After its own like working. A child's kiss*
> *Set on thy singing lips shall make thee glad;*
> *A poor man served by thee shall make thee rich;*
> *A sick man helped by thee shall make thee strong;*
> *Thou shalt be served thyself by every sense*
> *Of service which thou renderest."*
> **(Elizabeth Barrett Browning, "Reward of Service")**

our sovereignty over this fief, we can get back to the natural growth process from infant to child to adolescent to teen to young adult, not permitting truth to dazzle so quickly it destroys the soul.

In doing so, our first and most important responsibility will be to reestablish in our children what love really is.

She

"There is only one perfect flower in the wilderness of life.
   That flower is love.
There is only one fixed star in the mists of our wandering.
   That star is love.
There is only one hope in our despairing night.
   That hope is love.
All else is false. All else is shadow moving upon water.
   All else is wind and vanity.
Who shall say what is the weight or measure of love?
It is born of the flesh, it dwelleth in the spirit. From each
   doth it draw its comfort.
For beauty it is as a star.
Many are its shapes, but all are beautiful, and none know
   where the star rose, or the horizon where it shall set."
                                              —H. Rider Haggard

Love seems so simple—and it is. It is also complex. And since there are so many kinds of love, it cannot be a simple thing to arrive at general guidelines. Even C. S. Lewis was not able to reduce the many kinds to fewer than four in his book *The Four Loves*.

Many have tried to define it. Edwin Markham tried in eight lines.

Love's Dream
It cannot be uttered in speech,
 It quivers beyond the song:
However winged the phrase may be
 The words will do it wrong.

It can only be told in a glance,
 In the flash of a fleeting sign—
In the hidden spirit within a word
 That turns the water to wine.

Elizabeth Goudge tried to define it twice in her *Towers in the Mist:*

"It is always something . . . that brings joy; love of some human being, of beauty or of learning. Love is the unchanging landscape . . . at which, among the changes and chances of this mortal life, we sometimes look through the peep-hole of joy; and we have the love of God, of which human love is but a tiny echo—to be lost in it will be to have eternal life."

"Love is an unchanging thing, not an emotion but an element in which the whole world has its being. All the lovely things upon earth, beauty and truth and courage . . . are faint pictures of it, even as the puddles of rainwater capture a faint reproduction of a fiery sky bending over the earth."

But Goudge reduced it to its essence in *The Dean's Watch:*

"Love. The only indestructible thing. The only wealth and the only reality. The only survival. At the end of it all there is nothing else."

Victor Hugo in *Les Misérables*, perhaps the single greatest novel ever written, observed that "all of God's works were made to serve love. Love is powerful enough to charge all nature with its messages. . . . The future belongs still more to the heart than the mind. To love is the only thing that can occupy and fill up eternity. The infinite requires the inexhaustible. . . . Love partakes of the soul itself. It is of the same nature. Like the soul, it is a divine spark; it is incorruptible, indivisible, imperishable."

Love as Hollywood defines it is sadly at odds with the definitions we have just shared, for Hollywood's love is not love at all, but lust. Hollywood's love has not even nuances of divine love in its makeup. This media hub and its storytellers realize not that even human love is woefully incomplete without God to complete it, without God to anchor it in more than the marshy shallows of mere feelings.

Hollywood's love is full of qualifiers—just as is the love portrayed in popular music, its message very close to this: "We'll sing in the sunshine, we'll laugh in the rain; we'll enjoy the good-times—and then, I'll be on my way." In other words, don't even think of commitment to anything or anyone beyond mere feelings.

Harry Moyle Tippett, one of the greatest teachers of the first half of the twentieth century, described it thus in *Key in Your Hand:* "Love in its essence is without qualification. It is an absolute like chastity. And like chastity, love vanishes with its violation."

That is a message our amoral media has yet to learn: certainly it should have learned it by now, after untold celluloid portrayals of the violation of chastity followed by the vanishing of the love which supposedly preceded the forced sexual act.

Hollywood does not even leave us Edison Marshall's spar: "Love is a spar to cling to when everything else is gone, the most important and the greatest blessing of all" *(The Isle of Retribution).*

In Hollywood, love cannot be depended on to bring you through to safety. Nor is Hollywood's love anything at all like Hannah Moore's unselfish giving: "Love gives, gives like a thoughtless prodigal its all, and trembles then lest it has done too little."

Neither has Hollywood learned the lessons Dolly Roth Grey spoke of: "The more we love, the more we suffer. And yet it's all life, and the richness and fullness of life. If there were no valleys, there would be no mountaintops, and it's only by pain and suffering that one can taste the fullness of joy and happiness."

And in a second letter to her husband, Zane Grey, she wrote: "I have learned loving is giving, not demanding. Just to love deeply and greatly is uplifting and ennobling and brings its own reward, whether there be gratification or not."

That is yet another reality that the media fail to perceive. Gratification is not synonymous with deep, enduring, Christ-centered love. It has been a long time since Hollywood reflected the values that once undergirded its finest films, films such as *Tale of Two Cities, It's a Wonderful Life, Quo Vadis? The Robe, Ben Hur, A Man Called Peter, To Kill a Mockingbird, The Diary of Anne Frank, The Old Man and the Sea*, etc.

And in terms of love as reflected in our own behavior, if we will reread the Gospels and study our Lord's recorded words, we will discover that caring was what His earthly ministry was all about. In our lives, the only thing that registers on God's Richter scale is caring . . . loving others as He loves us.

We will need to find stories—we will discover many in Scripture—that will assist us in building within our children this supreme objective: a loving nature. There are many other such stories to be found if we will only take the time to search for them. These stories—read and reread, discussed, and referred to—will gradually translate into a Christ-centered, love-centered philosophy of life, just as what our children are currently being exposed to turns them into amoral, passive, or violent hedonists.

Of all that has been written about the higher level of love during the past several millenniums, there are four voices that we should pay particular attention to.

The first, C. S. Lewis's *Four Loves*, offers us invaluable guidelines that will greatly help us in our own interactions with others and as we seek divine wisdom in raising our children.

The second was penned in the twelfth century and is the finest and most succinct Christian philosophy of love in action outside of Holy Writ. It is the beloved prayer of Saint Francis of Assisi. The words, which have served as beacon lights of what we ought to be for eight centuries now, are these:

"Lord,
    Make me an instrument of Your peace.
    Where there is hatred let me sow love;
    Where there is injury, pardon;
    Where there is doubt, faith;
    Where there is despair, hope;
    Where there is darkness, light; and
    Where there is sadness, joy.

"O divine Master,
　Grant that I not so much
　Seek to be consoled as to console;
　To be understood as to understand;
　To be loved as to love;
　For it is in giving that we receive;
　It is in pardoning that we are pardoned; and
　It is in dying that we are born to eternal life."

The third voice is that of our Lord as revealed through Scripture, especially in the four Gospels. In them we have portrayed, moment by moment, the greatest love story of all time. Were we to spend just a tithe of the time we today devote to the media to a continual prayerful reading and rereading of the four Gospels, our lives and those of our children would be radically changed, and we would, over time, grow into His likeness.

Fourth, if we were deprived of the entire Bible and had but one chapter to live by—one chapter that reduced into a few verses the very essence of God's love and how we may reflect it—it would be the thirteenth chapter of the apostle Paul's first letter to the church at Corinth.

Each of us, of course, has our preferred translation, each with its own beauty and power. For timeless ringing beauty, it is unlikely any will ever improve on the King James translation. Of the modern translations, my two favorites are J. B. Phillips and *The New English Bible*, with a very slight edge going to the latter:

"I may speak in tongues of men or angels, but if I am without love, I am a sounding gong or a clanging cymbal. I may have the gift of prophecy, and know every hidden truth; I may have faith strong enough to move mountains; but if I have no love, I am nothing. I may dole out all I possess, or even give my body to be burnt, but if I have no love, I am none the better.

"Love is patient; love is kind and envies no one. Love is never boastful, nor conceited, nor rude; never selfish, not quick to take offence. Love keeps no score of wrongs; does not gloat over other men's sins, but delights in the truth. There is nothing love cannot face; there is no limit to its faith, its hope, and its endurance.

"Love will never come to an end. Are there prophets? their work will be over. Are there tongues of ecstasy? they will cease. Is there knowledge? it will vanish away; for our knowledge and our prophecy alike are partial, and the partial vanishes when wholeness comes. When I was a child, my speech, my outlook, and my thoughts were all childish. When I grew up, I had finished with childish things. Now we see only puzzling reflections in a mirror, but then we shall see face to face. My knowledge now is partial; then it will be whole, like God's knowledge of me. In a word, there are three things that last for ever: faith, hope, and love; but the greatest of them all is love" (1 Cor. 13, NEB).

CHAPTER 18

God Himself Can't Kill Them

"Boys flying kites haul in their white-winged birds;
You can't do that when you're flying words.
'Careful with fire' is good advice we know;
'Careful with words' is ten times doubly so.
Thoughts unexpressed may sometimes fall back dead,
But God Himself can't kill them once they're said"
(Will Carleton, "First Settler's Story").

Our family has long utilized these powerful concluding lines
from Will Carleton's frontier story poem as a warning to
our careless use of words—especially in terms of wounding those dear to us. But these lines have a wider application as
well: Words appear to embody more long-term ability to serpent-
like attack again and again than does mere visual imagery. These
words are like venom-filled fangs, as the pain caused by the attack
abrasions are minor compared to the automatic venom release
caused by contact with flesh.

Just as this cause-and-effect is operable with words meant to
wound, just so are they with words incorporated into vicariously
experienced media programming. Although the adult viewer can
experience drama on two levels, (1) knowing it's not true but (2)
responding to it as if it really were true, the body's nervous system
is no different from what it was when, as a child, what was seen on
the screen was perceived as actual reality. The nervous system, not
being subject to the mind's sway very much, is just as emotionally
affected by what is being vicariously experienced as by what is
actually being experienced in real life. This is the reason so many
heavy viewers of soap operas have severe marital problems: they
are so drained by the vicarious reliving of the drama that they have
very little left to give to the husband or wife in real life.

And once these vicariously experienced video scenes are recorded in the mind's archives, from then on the individual in future
years will have difficulty deciding which imagery was actually
experienced and which was experienced secondhand. Both—with
all the attendant violence or obscene language—are now safely

stored within, subject to recall upon reflex or demand. Both have the capacity either to gild or darken the skies of the subconscious. The sad truth is this: if a man and woman have a near-idyllic marriage, including a mutually satisfying and fulfilling physical relationship, and if one of the partners is daily recording cinematic relationships, many of which prove to be unsatisfactory and pain-ridden, over time gradually those "unreal" experiences will begin to cloud, distort, cheapen, and eventually wreck the real. And so it destroys the marriage itself!

The other side of the coin is just as bad. Since most cinema sexual relationships are glamorized and sensationalized, far more so than would be true in real life, over time the hero or heroine synthesizes into such a symbol of perfection or sexual prowess that no person in real life could possibly, over time, match it. As a result, the viewer loses interest in the spouse, and another marriage is history.

Marriage counselors more and more are blaming television for marriage breakups. One of the principal problems is that, when the tube is on, it is very difficult for the spouses to hold a normal discussion about anything.

We have all noticed the truth of the aphorism "Two's company, three's a crowd." In real life two children may play amicably together for hours, but rarely will the same be true where three are concerned. When husband and wife are alone together in comparative silence, communication is likely to occur, at least on an intermittent basis. But let a friend—a friend of hers or a friend of his—ring the doorbell and come in . . . and the conversation variables are radically different!

The same is true with the television set. When off, it exerts no more influence than a piece of furniture. But on, it becomes a guest, an obnoxious guest that selfishly monopolizes all conversation. Meaningful conversation will not be possible until it is finally turned off. Many are the instances in which one of the partners consistently uses the set as a third-party friend in order to avoid interaction. And it is so easy to do: The moment the spouse walks in the door, on comes the set—not to be turned off until one or both are too tired to talk to each other. Just as it is true that many spouses fall out of love and friendship with each other and don't realize it until the last child leaves home and the resulting silence brings home to them the realization that, without the children, they no longer have anything in common . . . just so, constant TV intrusion can obscure—until it is too late to remedy—the reality that the set is the only factor that is keeping them within the same four walls. The friendship itself has been lost by default because one partner obviously values what is said on TV more than what the spouse might say, given the chance to do so.

One key reason for continued dialogue is that, each day of our lives, each partner is changing—is becoming something other than what she or he was. Sadly, many marriages founder because one or both partners still conceptualize the other in terms of what once was rather than what is. Only as each keeps falling in love—or like—with the other as the journey through life proceeds is there much of a chance that the bond will survive the seismic shocks life has in store down the line.

Television is the chief gremlin in the conversational machinery of life. Not only that, but the more one or both watch the tube, the less one will admire the other. Talents will inevitably atrophy, and projects and growth will never be achieved. And marriage without genuine respect for each other rarely endures for long.

Wilford A. Peterson, writing about the power of words, observed: "Soft words sung in a lullaby will put a babe to sleep. Excited words will stir a mob to violence. Eloquent words will send armies marching into the face of death. Encouraging words will fan to flame the genius of a Rembrandt or a Lincoln. Powerful words will mold the public mind as the sculptor molds his clay. Words are a dynamic force. . . . When you speak, when you write, remember the creative power of words" ("Words Go Marching On," *Sunshine*, Feb. 1966).

"Words are the swords we use in our battle for success and happiness. How others react toward us depends, in a large measure, upon the words we speak to them. Life is a great whispering gallery that sends back echoes of the words we send out! Our words are immortal, too. They go marching through the years in the lives of all those with whom we come in contact" (Wilford A. Peterson, "Words Go Marching On," Sunshine, Feb. 1966).

But as significant as are words in the lives of adults, they are far more so in the life of a child. During the five years I directed

Southwestern Adventist College's Adult Degree Program in Texas, we shared several hundred life stories as we wrestled with autobiographies. The lesson which hit home over and over was that the words which were said to these individuals—then ranging in age from 20 to 80—whether said 1, 5, 10, 20, 50, or 75 years before were indelibly etched in their memory banks.

When the gates of memory were pushed ajar by chain-association, they would remember—remember when an authority figure (parent, teacher, minister, etc.) told them in cutting or slashing words that they were of little worth and never would be worth much. Why couldn't they be like X or Y or Z? These words, said in the heat of who knows what pressure factor, gradually took control of that part of the psyche which has to do with self-worth—and for many who shared these stories they became self-fulfilling prophecies. Because they were told they were of little value,

**"A word is dead
When it is said,
Some say.**

**I say it just
Begins to live
That day"
(Emily Dickinson).**

they believed it; because they believed it, they failed to achieve and thus became of little value—and so confirmed those blighting words!

So it is that we must guard our lips extra carefully where children are concerned. When we err, we should always err on the side of building up rather than tearing down. For, if we fail to do so, a half century later our terrible words may still be lashing a could-have-been-success to an ever more tragic and needless failure.

CHAPTER 19

That Most Misunderstood Quality: Creativity

Just what does it mean to be creative? I submit that we have many misconceptions that block us from achieving very much. Most of us appear to believe that only certain "gifted," college-educated people have this trait. The truth of the matter is that the educational process itself is probably the greatest enemy the creative muse has. Just think about that horrifying statistic mentioned earlier: preschoolers before TV—97-100 percent creativity; high school graduates—2-3 percent creativity. An incredible flip-flop during the first 12 years of formal education! Sadly, all too often our children and youth are taught to doubt their own powers, their own voice. Unless Dr. So-and-So from X university says it's so, it ain't. Now, that's tragic! It represents one of the most frustrating problems I face in the college classroom. I ask a student what he or she thinks and that student turns the tables on me: "You tell me first. What do *you* think, Dr. Wheeler?" Far too often our education consists of mere regurgitation of what the teacher dishes out. Since students will remember, at best, 18 percent of what they knew for a test one week ago, regurgitation is dead-end learning. We can learn only by continual reinforcement . . . and by a passionate interest in what we are studying. I view teaching, as did Oliver Wendell Holmes, as a standing side-by-side with the student, facing this exciting world the Lord has entrusted to us and exploring it together as partners—not master and servant. After all, a Ph.D.—despite the way some of us act—does not automatically bring with it the gift of omniscience.

Creativity to me is in essence just believing in your God-given voice. That's what I try to hammer home in my classes: "God entrusted *each* of you with a unique way of looking at life and reality. No one else has ever taken, can take, or will take your place . . . for only *you* perceive with the vision that is unique to you alone."

I can never forget a moment out of one of my first years of teaching. Jeannie was her name. When asked to write in her seven-minute notebook, her eyes blazed: "How can I write? *Nothing* ever happens to me!" Years later we met again. She and her husband were furloughing from mission service on the Amazon, and how we laughed at her earlier words.

> *"All around us are people whose eyes are full of light but who see nothing in sea or sky, nothing in city streets, nothing in books. It were far better to sail forever in the night of blindness with sense, and feeling, and mind, than to be content with the mere act of seeing. The only lightless dark is the night of darkness in ignorance and insensitivity"* (Helen Keller).

The reality is that every moment of our lives has meaning. Virginia Woolf gave graphic proof of that when she was able to make a riveting story out of "The Death of a Moth." What is missing in our lives is not the raw material or the incidents themselves, but the awareness of them. And the media has stolen that from us as well by their sensationalizing, robbing us of the capacity to appreciate the commonplace acts of life, robbing us of the beauty of all that is less than spectacular.

People consider me creative because I write. People consider my concert artist brother Romayne creative because he performs, composes music, and writes poetry. People consider my father creative because he paints pictures. They say my father-in-law is creative because of his uniquely beautiful fireplaces, turrets, and houses. But creativity includes much more than writing, composing, painting, or performing.

My wife, Connie, and her mother have created a long line of quilts. In fact, at any given moment the chances are excellent that my wife is working on one. Each of these quilts represents a portion of her life and energy and bears her own unique signature of individuality. For almost two years now she has been slowly creating one of those intricate marvels of quiltdom, a "grandma's flower garden." She still has three or four years to go before it's likely to be finished. That quilt is every bit as much an expression of her creativity as my writing this book, and it is likely to bring beauty, love, warmth, and comfort for a century or more!

My mother is creative in many ways, especially with the spoken word. But she is also extremely creative as a cook. In fact, she remembers holidays through the years not by what we did, but by what we ate! She remembers exact menus 10, 20, 30 years ago! "Oh, that was the Christmas we had that most delicious, unparalleled lemon pie . . ." And she will float away in rapture at the mere salivating thought! When I was at Southwestern Adventist College, directing the Community Lyceum Series, one program was different from all else. We featured the José Vasques family—had them cater Tex-Mex food from their restaurant and perform Latino music—and then we surprised them with testimonials, live and otherwise, from the local mayor to state senator to state governor to U.S. senator to President and Mrs. Ronald Reagan. I'd venture to say that, until that memorable evening, many in our audience had not realized how creative the culinary art can be. To plan a menu, with visual as well as taste appeal, to decorate the table and room, to set a mood by lighting and music—now, that's creativity!

Here and there in my own life I have been fortunate enough to encounter an individual who has made of friendship a fine art. One of these is a wonderful young-at-heart lady, Helen Mallicoat, of Wickenburg, Arizona. Not only is her writing loved and appreciated everywhere, not only does she make about 50 quilts a year to give away, but she also finds time to keep up a far-reaching skein of correspondence. She has made of all three—writing, quiltmaking, and correspondence—fine arts.

Then there was my own patron saint, Dr. Walter Utt, of Pacific Union College, who made of mentoring an art comparable to that of Titian. He somehow saw something in each of us that no one else saw . . . and he let us know that he saw it. No one knows how many hundreds of individuals gained confidence in their own voice, in their own creativity, just because he believed in them—not just that, but he kept at it steadily until his last breath.

Then there are those who love to garden. My maternal grandmother took a rock-studded hill in California's Napa Valley region and, by dint of dawn-to-dusk weeding, hoeing, watering, and loving, transformed the spot into a garden paradise—every bit as much a work of art as a Brussels tapestry. Or it may be that one's talents lie in areas such as wood, metal, ceramics, glass; within these media, the individual creates masterpieces. And we have all known people such as my sister Marjorie Wheeler-Raymond who can take a weed here, a weed there, a long-stemmed flower or two, a small branch, some sprigs of fern, some dry grass—and from it create a centerpiece so stunning it takes the breath away. An interior decorator starts with four walls and, with an eye for what "could be," transforms that box into a breath of spring. And there are architects such as the famed Frank Lloyd Wright, who took a Pennsylvania hillside, a creek, some stone, steel, wood, glass, and mortar . . . and made of it that timeless vision of beauty, "Falling Water."

So not one of us can validly claim we are doomed to a dead-end media-saturated life because we are culturally deprived, have no artistic talents at all—because it simply isn't true.

Perhaps your creative fulfillment will come from finding single parents who are desperately struggling to juggle a low-paying job, a second job, children, housework, yard upkeep, cooking, etc., and are sinking under the totality of it all. Your helping hand would probably be considered heaven-sent. Perhaps it would be a ministry to those forgotten senior citizens among us who never receive any visitors at the rest home and are yearning for a friend.

There are so many things each of us could do to lighten the burdens of others, so many ways we can grow, develop talents and skills. The potential for growth, service, and fulfillment is everywhere around us.

All we have to do is open our eyes.

But we must do more than open our eyes. We must act as well. For some mysterious reason, the Creator has seen fit to provide us with kaleidoscopic inner vision: No two images, no two perceptions, no two impulses, no two urges, no two moments of insight or vision, are ever exactly alike. Thus, the penalty of failing to act on an inner urge, failing to write that line of prose that rings like a golden bell, failing to write that letter of solace, is to never again achieve what was in our grasp for that one elusive moment.

CHAPTER 20

◆

The Rabbi's Eight Magic Words

As I look back on that memorable evening more than a quarter century ago, it still seems nigh unto incredible to me that one speech could change a person's life. From birth to the grave we are so bombarded with words, words, words that after a while we develop almost an immunity to them.

Up until that memorable evening I was—like so many of my acquaintances—not much better than a drifter. I did my job quite well, but there is a vast difference between "quite well" and "very well." I was teaching English classes from early in the morning until late in the afternoon, and at night I would correct papers and watch TV. My life was taking on a deadly gray tinge as I began to sink deeper into the ruts of my own making: drag myself out of bed, gulp down breakfast, hurry off to school, teach class after class after class all day, return home in time for supper, correct the never-ending stream of themes (which are the cross of English teachers everywhere), watch a number of hours of TV, and turn it off only when I finally shuffled off to bed.

Several years went by, and the pattern of my life remained virtually unchanged. Intellectually I stagnated. In this treadmill of frenetic movement, I felt like Alice in Wonderland, who, puffing away after her strenuous race with the Red Queen, rather plaintively observes that, despite all the exertion, they seem to be right where they started from. Running fast and getting nowhere—intellectually, physically, or spiritually—that was me.

"How would you like to take in a speech tonight?"

"You've got to be kidding! Not on your life . . . Uh . . . where? . . . Who?"

"The apostle Richard Evans of the Mormon Church."

The mention of his name brought back fond memories of the magnificent Tabernacle organ, the awesome Mormon Tabernacle Choir, and "the spoken word by Richard Evans" every Sunday morning "from the crossroads of the West." During the summers I worked in Utah I tried to get to the broadcast as often as I possibly could. As for Evans, he easily had one of the greatest, most sonorous speaking voices I have ever been privileged to hear. The combination of the organ, the choir, and that voice would send chills up my spine.

Every tired bone in my body fought against venturing out on that cold winter night just to hear a speech. But those warm memories were too strong

" 'Well, in our country,' said Alice, still panting a little, 'you'd generally get to somewhere else—if you ran very fast for a long time as we've been doing.'

" 'A slow sort of country!' said the Queen. 'Now, here, you see, it takes all the running you can do, to keep in the same place. If you want to get somewhere else, you must run at least twice as fast as that!' " (Lewis Carroll, Through the Looking-Glass).

to fight, so we braved the cold and, with God's help, things have never been the same since.

There in the Ambassador's Club a large crowd had gathered, in spite of the cold weather outside. With some difficulty we finally found seats.

Evans stood up, as I had seen him do so many times before, but this time it was different. Oh, it was the same voice. It flowed like warm honey into every crevice of your being. And, as always, it was obvious that here was a deeply sincere man who had a close relationship with his God. Always a master of the dramatic effect, he stood there for what seemed to us like forever, in complete silence—just looking at us intently, his eyes scanning the large audience. Then he announced to us just what he was going to do with us during the hour—always a dangerous thing to do with an audience, for we tend to perversely dig our heels into the ground when this is done, and say, in effect, "Over my dead body, you will."

So . . . he was going to change our lives with just eight little words. How ridiculous can anyone get! And certainly *I* scoffed—a veteran of scores of Weeks of Spiritual Emphasis and several thousand sermons and talks. If *they* hadn't made a radical change in me, just how, pray tell, was Evans going to do it with eight measly little words?

But despite my Sarah-like chuckling behind the door, I listened. We all listened because, deep down in most of us, was a hazy awareness that we lacked that vital spark that separates the living from the dead . . . the spark Evans had and we didn't.

There was another dramatic pause . . . a long hush. Then, very quietly, Evans began. In essence, these were his key points: Most of us procrastinate our way through life and consequently accomplish very little that is worthwhile or will leave much of an impact after we are gone. He certainly had us there. We stirred restlessly, and surreptitiously looked around us to see if the others looked guilty as well. Satisfied that the condition was general, we listened even more intently.

Why were we in such a condition? Because we were failing to organize well the most precious commodity God has given us—time! Most of us, reminded Evans, are little more than robots who unthinkingly use up the 25,000 days—that is an average, not a guarantee—flesh is heir to. We tend to delude ourselves by imagining that there will always be plenty of extra time someday, time to accomplish then all the things we are not getting done today. So it is, declared Evans in his most serious and solemn tone, that hour after hour, day after day, week after week, month after month, and year after year is frittered away. Why? Because we have failed to take seriously the truth that seconds, minutes, and hours eventually translate into the years of our lives.

I looked around again; almost no one else was. Evidently the shoe was pinching the others as well, each thinking, *He's talking about me.* Faces, rosy in hue, looked straight ahead. There was another pause, and then: "Friends, these are the magic words that will change your life:

If not now—when?
If not me—whom?"

He went on to answer our unspoken question. Just how can these simple little words change my life? First of all, he admonished us, we must repeat these eight words over and over to ourselves, repeat them all day long and into the night, repeat them all week, and during the rest of the month—and then, at a lessening pace throughout the year, not stopping until they become part of the very fiber of our beings. From that time on, they would operate on the subconscious level.

He reminded us that the Library of Congress had about 10 million titles (there are double that today!). And since each of our lives would consist in no small part of the quality books we had read and were reading, it behooved us to get in there and read!

Evans then got tough with us, accusing us of murdering time and thereby shortcutting our own spiritual and intellectual growth by reading either mental pablum or debased reading material.

He wasn't through yet—not by a long shot! In retrospect, it seems amazing to me that, way back in the mid-sixties, Evans had a prophetic vision of how television would destroy the very soul of this nation. TV, he declared, was far and above the greatest waste of time the world had ever known. Families that once read together and interacted with each other now sat glued to the idiot box, the one-eyed bandit. He solemnly warned us that on judgment day each one of us was going to have to answer for all the time we spent before the TV, hypnotized by its spell.

Then he seemed to relax and observed, "The things you watch may not necessarily be evil, but if they accomplish nothing other than to entertain constantly, they might as well be evil, for your minds will be the losers." Twelve hours a week was the amount of time we were wasting! Today I think back to that moment and wonder what he would have thought if he could see what is being shown today—and for good measure know that we are now watching two and a half times that many hours every week.

Evans returned to the attack. Books: we always think we have plenty of time to read them . . . down the line somewhere. "Do you know how many books you are likely to read in a lifetime?" We didn't know: obviously thousands. Well, he said, let's say we are really conscientious—reading a book a week. How good we are! "Add it up," advised Evans. Let's see, a book a week adds up to 52 books a year, 520 in 10 years. In 70 years that would be 3,640 books. But he stopped us in our tracks. "How old are you now? How much time have you already lost?" Thanks to some quick mental arithmetic, I was sobered to discover that I only had, at a book a week, about 2,860 left that I was likely to read. And since even in the mid-sixties there were close to 20,000 new titles being added yearly, my paltry 2,860 wouldn't enable me to keep up with even one year's books, much less make much of a dent on the vast amount of reading already out there. "In fact, friends, in your entire lifetime, at a book a week, you'll only read about a sixth of the books published in this one year!" To have kept up with the publishing *then*, we would have had to read at least a book a day. "So, friends, you have no time either to read or watch trash!"

I went home a very sober man.

I determined to give it a try, on the twin premises that I didn't have anything to lose, and that I had been told many times that "with God, all things are possible."

Later on I discovered that the eight magic words did not originate with Evans. They dated back 2,000 years to Rabbi Hillel of the first century (70 B.C.-A.D. 10), who is considered to be one of the greatest rabbis of all time. In fact, it is interesting to note how much his philosophy of life meshes with that of Christ as He taught the people.

As for me, that night represents the Rubicon between what I was at that time and what I have become since.

Practically, how do the words work? Let me illustrate. Your small child breaks through the wall of your concentration while attempting to secure your full attention. In instances such as this, many of us would likely shunt the child off on a siding. Chances are he or she is asking a question imbued with eternal significance: questions such as Who is Jesus? Do you know Him? What is God like? How good do I have to be to go to heaven?

If you don't answer these questions when your child is interested in receiving an answer, he or she may never ask them again, or may ask someone else, perhaps someone whose answer may differ radically from yours. If these eight words have become truly a part of you, you will respond to the child's search for meaning by asking yourself, "If not now—when?" If you don't answer this question now, when, if ever, will you answer it? Will it be asked again? Will your answer mean as much years from now?

The result should be that, stopping everything else, you will give the child your undivided attention.

Perhaps some time ago you were asked to write an article but have been procrastinating. The eight magic words will force you to a decision. If you are honest in response to "If not now—when?" you will have to admit that, since most of us follow the path of least resistance, we are likely to procrastinate. Being aware of this helps us energize our vital forces and do the job in question.

The "If not me—whom?" question should bring home the realization that either the article will not be written or someone else will be asked to do it. It will then be too late for you to make your own unique contribution.

Every time we are urged to accomplish something and fail to do it, we are weaker. The other side of the coin is that every time we overcome inertia and create, we are henceforth measurably stronger. Over a long period of time our personal response to these eight words will result in tangible differences in our character.

When we are asked to help out in church activities, be it in the primary, junior, youth, or adult division, the usual response from many of us is no. However, applying the "If not now—when?" part of the formula results in our admitting that this postponement of personal involvement is likely to become a chronic rather than a transient condition, with attendant weakening of our fiber.

The "If not me—whom?" question forces us to explore alternatives: Who are the next most likely candidates for accepting the responsibility we rejected? Are they as qualified for the job? Will they do as well as we would have? Are these others already overburdened? What will our rejection do to our own psyches? Again, it is probable that applying the eight words will cause us to assume our own fair share of responsibility.

Most of us are lazy readers. Either we don't read at all or we absorb a steady diet of mental pablum. In my case, "If not now—when?" forced me to admit that I was unlikely to read heavyweight material unless forced to by an external source. I rationalized that after dealing with ideas and academics five days a week I needed a change of pace in the evenings. Of course, this "relaxing" reading had no energizing effect at all on me, for it was merely escapism. After a long dialogue with myself, I reached a compromise. The compromise takes the form of a game: for every lightweight, I must take on a heavyweight. The result is that I have finally read many dust-covered classics heretofore exiled to my shelves. When we realize how limited our time for reading is in a lifetime, it ill behooves us to waste our time on trash or trivia.

Most of us seemingly assume that there will always be time tomorrow to do the things we've long talked about doing. For instance, how many times have we considered taking the children for a vacation? Yet we always find excuses, such as not having enough time or money. But when we come to grips with the situation, we discover that we generally have the time and money for what we really want to do.

We note that the children are rapidly growing up; soon they

won't even want to go with us on family vacations. So we go, and are forever grateful that we did, for it brings a new closeness to the children and leaves us with enough fond memories to last a lifetime.

The magic words need to be used also for the small actions of life, because the seemingly insignificant actions of life add up to major habit patterns. Suppose that as you are about to leave for work you spy a pair of socks on the floor. You ask, "If not now—when?" and respond by "Probably later, if they are still there when I return from work." The "If not me—whom?" question results in your admitting that your long-suffering wife will probably see them and feel forced to pick them up. Realistically, you realize that such a default on your part will not cause your spouse's love for you to grow—rather, it will likely blight it. Many, many marriages go into tailspins because one or both parties cease showing their best sides to the other, assuming—with disastrous results—that once they are married the worst side of their natures can safely be displayed to the other. The inescapable result that comes from applying the eight words is that you pick up those socks.

Practicing the golden rule has smoothed many a road during my lifetime, whereas failure to do so has resulted in washboard-road whiplash.

They will change your life. Make them yours too.

If not now—when?
If not me—whom?

Special Note

If I ever doubted the leading of a Higher Power in the evolution of this book, that question had its lid slammed on it when, in poring through a lifetime's worth of files, I stumbled on the original notes I had taken at the Ambassador's Club more than a quarter century ago! Through the years, as I had ransacked my files for articles and lectures on the subject, they had never surfaced before—and now, when they were most needed, here they were! I could only bow my head and gratefully pray, "Thank You, Lord."

CHAPTER 21

Do Not Go Gentle Into That Good Night

Youth is not a time of life. . . . It is a state of mind. It is not a matter of ripe cheeks, red lips and supple knees. It is a temper of the will, a quality of the imagination, a vigor of the emotions; it is a freshness in the deep springs of life.

"Youth means a temperamental predominance of courage over timidity, of the appetite for adventure over love of ease. This often exists in the man of 50 more than the boy of 20.

"Nobody grows old by merely living a number of years. People grow old by deserting their ideals. Years wrinkle the skin, but self distrust, fear and despair . . . those are the long, long years that bow the head and turn the growing spirit back to dust.

"You are as young as your faith, as old as your doubt; as young as your self-confidence, as old as your fear; as young as your hope, as old as your despair.

"In the central part of your heart there is a wireless station. So long as it receives messages of beauty, hope, cheer, courage, grandeur and power from the earth, from man or woman, and from the infinite, so long are you young. . . . When the wires are all down and the central part of your heart is covered with the snows of pessimism and the ice of cynicism, then you are grown old indeed and may God have mercy on your soul" (Author Unknown; quoted in a Josephine Lowman column).

I have been luckier than most: a minister father who at 82 continues to turn out painting after painting, works vigorously every day in his garden, puts on variety hours with my mother at churches and schools all over the Northwest, and still finds time to preach almost every Sabbath! He and my indefatigable mother set a pace that leaves many younger people panting behind. They daily continue to memorize an ever larger number of biblical verses. For recreation, they visit rest homes where people 10 to 20 years their junior, glassy-eyed as they sit there before TV sets, are vegetating out of life—dying before their time. People say that at 82 Dad is preaching the best sermons of his lifetime . . . and he sings without that old age quaver. And my wife's father, a contractor in Texas, is every bit as active. Even I, with difficulty, can keep up with his pace of work.

Nothing more graphically reveals to me the difference from what we once were and what we have become than just remembering Grandpa. And nothing reveals more vividly the catastrophic loss of creativity and individuality America has experienced during the past half-century than remembering Grandpa.

Once upon a time, before television pulverized individuality, there were millions who were just as unique in their way as was Grandpa—and upon this treasure house of creativity was built the greatest nation in the world. Today, we are increasingly hard-pressed—no small thanks to TV—to find originals at all.

Yes, looking back in time, one figure stands out against the years in bold relief: my maternal grandfather, Herbert Norton Lininger. A man of strong likes and dislikes, who always stood tall and ramrod straight, he was exciting to be around. The walls of the house were papered with *National Geographic* maps so that he could keep up with the news as the global field commander he envisioned himself to be. I was fortunate enough to spend one entire year with my grandparents—my eighth grade year—and that one year had a profound impact on my life.

Adjacent to the house and sloping down to the highway were the several acres of plants which made Grandpa's nursery business possible. Behind the house was a redwood forest, which I would frequently prowl. How passing strange it is to go back now and see how small the forest really was—but to my adolescent eyes then, it stretched away to forever. One reason I loved it there was that the house was full of books—and my grandparents bought more just for me. In the evenings, when the house was still, I'd go up to my attic eyrie, stretch out on my bed by the window, read until the wee hours of the morning, watch the ghostly headlights of cars traveling up and down Highway 101 in the fog—Arcata, California, was seemingly almost *always* foggy!—and dream . . . dream of what my life might bring.

On holidays, the family would gather from far and near, and Grandpa would tread the boards of the front room, his stage, reciting Shakespeare and Kipling by the hour, and giving his state of the world addresses, striding energetically all over the west end of the big house, pointing to places on maps where things were happening, and railing against the crooks in Washington who let them. Of course, this never kept him from writing government officials, alerting them to where they had zigged when they should have zagged . . . or occasionally even awarding them the Herbert Lininger Award of Good Conduct if they had actually behaved themselves.

Grandma had learned many years before that if she was going to wait and speak when the Lord of the Manor paused for breath, she might as well never talk at all, for Grandpa, once he captured an audience, never took breaths, for a millisecond pause might enable one of his squirming captive sons-in-law to—perish the thought!—sneak a word in edgewise. Grandpa considered such an act from the younger generation to be cheeky, for he was, after all, the family oracle, with every word he spoke outweighing any five of theirs.

We children, there being no TV sets to siphon away our attention, sat on the floor, thoroughly enjoying the discomfiture of our own paternal authority figures, for once reduced to sputtering silence and aborted mutterings. On the other side of the room, Grandma too would have by this time hit her stride, informing the daughters (all five of them) about all the family and friend news—here, however, there was more give and take: the daughters gave as good as they took—and there was much laughter. On the floor, we had our own conversations going, meanwhile picking up both adult tracks of sight and sound as part of the general hubbub. In retrospect, it seems incredible that such a wild and wacky happening could ever have actually taken place, but I would guess that similar types of family get-togethers were anything but rare in those pre-TV days when American individualism still reigned supreme.

But, back to Grandpa. In spite of his jaundiced attitude toward the political animal, he had one patron saint: FDR. Grandpa never forgot that when he lost all of his money during the darkest days of the great Depression, and the family larder was almost empty, in sheer desperation, he had written Roosevelt asking—not for dole: that would have been unthinkable to Grandpa!—but for work. Within minutes, it always seemed to Grandpa in retrospect, from the moment the letter reached the White House, a call went out to a high Humboldt County official: *"Get Herbert Lininger a job!"* From that moment on, for Grandpa, FDR was absolved from all the sins politicians are naturally heir to.

Another thing we children loved in him was his childlike irrepressibility: He apparently always said whatever he felt like saying whenever the mood was upon him to do so—and the mood apparently never knew anything but a long succession of green lights, for Grandma rarely dared to signal so much as a yellow. Always, there was a bit of the impish, slightly naughty boy about him. In the midst of Kipling, he would look around surreptitiously to see if those guardians of our morals, our mothers, were listening, then would gracefully slide into the opening lines of "I Learned About Women From Her" and start his mental countdown to the first of his indignant daughters' "Oh Papa" . . . which he would, of course, studiously ignore and continue on, much to our delight. We, of course, didn't really understand just what there was about Kipling's poem to get our mothers so indignant . . . but we just thought it wonderful that Grandpa could repeat wicked things and get away with it, for we certainly couldn't.

To Grandpa, the world was one big adventure and a lifetime was far too short a period for exploring it. Thus I would hear the furnace come on while it was still dark every morning, hear Grandpa puttering around downstairs, and then the early morning news which set his sails for the day. If ever a man had a Falstaffian zest for life, it was Grandpa, for he felt it was his civic and Christian duty to explore every aspect and every sensation life had to offer. Food fell within this dispensation. Although Grandpa was baptized a Christian late in life, where biblical diet was concerned, he mule-headedly balked. And he continued to explore rare delicacies such as rattlesnake meat—which he pronounced "delicious." And how can I ever forget one weekend when Grandpa loaded the three of us into the car and took us up to a river where there were eels spawning? Unfortunately for Grandma and me, Grandpa had never yet tasted eel—hence he rounded up a bucketful and we headed home. Then he put the foul-smelling things on the stove and waited out the interminable period it took to reduce the nasty pus-yellow innards to a reasonably edible state. The stench was so bad that for three days Grandma and I bunked outside the house!

In his mid-seventies, he blithely announced that for 50 years he had pleased society and his wife by being clean-shaven. The time had now come for him to please himself . . . so he blossomed out with a moustache and a distinguished-looking goatee. It was also about this time that he decided it was high time to get away from his Penelope, and, like Ulysses, strike out for the great unknown. But first, he had to have a vessel and a fellow mariner. The chosen bark was a Studebaker pickup. Among his cronies was a luckless soul we knew only as "Mr. Smith." Grandpa enlisted him in the great venture, and together they began preparing the Studebaker for its future trials and tribulations. There was no such thing as a camper in those days. In fact, the monstrosity that Grandpa and Mr. Smith evolved was the first "camper" I ever remember seeing. The metal box they constructed was so long that it defied gravity: how the front wheels stayed on the road I'll never know! When they were all through, one thing remained to be done: paint it. Without a doubt, it must have been the bargain of the century: that paint—in all my life, I have never seen, before or since, a more hideous shade of pea-green! Satisfied with their artistic efforts, they stocked its bowels with enough grub, clothing, equipment, and et ceteras to equip San Francisco for a year—and headed north. We heard little from them as they were too busy exploring every side road separating them from the North Pole. Eventually, after more adventures than they ever enlightened us on, their faithful green beast balked at last: at the end of the northernmost road in the hemisphere. Unable to convince the understandably sulky Studebaker that it was amphibious, they reluctantly turned back.

Once home, Grandpa decided that the open road beat domesticity, so he and Mr. Smith began preparations for another expedition: this one south into the jungles of Mexico. And soon, the threesome pulled out onto 101 and headed toward the border. Again, they were gone a long time—and again, the stories were so many that even Grandpa could never retell them all.

Eventually, the era of the ugly green camper came to an end . . . and, in his eighties, Grandpa looked for new frontiers. Rivers were next. Mr. Smith by this time having pitched his last tent, Grandpa began exploring rivers from their sources down to the sea. Out of the mists of my youth is a strange image: a group of faithful family positioned on the banks of the Sacramento River.

Suddenly, excitedly, everyone points way off in the distance where an outboard-powered rubber raft piloted by a goateed explorer begins veering shoreward.

The exchange (refuse off and grubstake replenished on the cheap) completed as quickly as an Indy 500 tank-fill, he was away and heading downriver, turning back just once for a last jaunty wave.

The day of his death—in his mid-eighties—he was roaring all over the Oregon countryside in his Lincoln hardtop. His eyesight no longer what it once was, he and his Lincoln wiped out mailboxes right and left whenever they had the audacity to stray within range.

It was the only funeral I have ever attended where people laughed.

✦ ✦ ✦

Never can I think of Grandpa without calling to mind two poems: First, some ever so appropriate lines from one of Grandpa's favorite poems, Tennyson's "Ulysses."

"I cannot rest from travel; I will drink
  Life to the lees. All times I have enjoy'd
  Greatly, have suffer'd greatly, both with those
  That loved me, and alone; on shore, and when
  Thro' scudding drifts the rainy Hyades
  Vext the dim sea. I am become a name;
  For always roaming with a hungry heart
  Much have I seen and known,—cities of men,
  And manners, climates, councils, governments. . . .
  I am a part of all that I have met;
  Yet all experience is an arch wherethro'
  Gleams that untravell'd world whose margin fades
  For ever and for ever when I move.
  How dull it is to pause, to make an end,
  To rust, unburnish'd, not to shine in use!
  As tho' to breathe were life! Life piled on life
  Were all too little, and of one to me
  Little remains; but every hour is saved
  From that eternal silence, something more,

A bringer of new things; and vile it were
For some three suns to store and hoard myself,
And this gray spirit yearning in desire
To follow knowledge like a sinking star,
Beyond the utmost bound of human thought.

Far too often, the golden years turn out to be nightmare years instead in today's society. Perhaps it is because of a major misconception of how the body works. Why is it that those who determine to wear out rather than rust out live so much longer? In this respect, the two most significant statements I have ever come across came my way during the years in which I directed South-western Adventist College's Adult Degree Program. The first: "Senility can be postponed almost indefinitely, provided the individual continues to dream, grow, and work toward new goals."

And the second: "The average individual dies seven years after retirement."

Studies have repeatedly confirmed that these dictums are more than rhetoric: a 65-year-old retiree does tend to die by 72; a 40-year-old retiree by 47; and a 90-year-old retiree by 97. It seems that when the brain signals the white armies of blood cells with the momentous news that all the dreams and goals that a person has been living for are now in the past, the white blood cells accept that message as a signal that peace has come at last; it is time to disarm. When that occurs, it is only a matter of time before death claims its own. The only exceptions are senior citizens like my grandfather and my parents who continually dream new dreams, set new goals, and enthusiastically set out to make them come true.

They are the literal embodiment of the filial message in Dylan Thomas' poetic urging in "Do Not Go Gentle Into That Good Night," from which come the following lines:

"Do not go gentle into that good night,
  Old age should burn and rave at close of day;
  Rage, rage against the dying of the light.
  Though wise men at their end know dark is night
  Because their words had forked no lightning they
  Do not go gentle into that good night. . . .

And you, my father, there on the sad height,
Curse, bless, me now with your fierce tears, I pray.
Do not go gentle into that good night.
Rage, rage against the dying of the light."
(Dylan Thomas: *Poems of Dylan Thomas*. Copyright 1952 by
Dylan Thomas. Reprinted by permission of New Directions
Publishing Corp.).

One of the saddest geriatric news bulletins of our time has to
do with the growing number of couples who divorce *after* they
have lived together for almost half a century—usually, not long
after retirement. Scholars studying the phenomenon are convinced
there are several reasons. Up until retirement, husband and wife
have remained busy in their respective careers and other involvements, consequently they have continued to visualize each other as
productive and creative; but, after retirement, they suddenly
experience more of each other than they wish to handle. It appears
that we are not fashioned to either need or desire non-stop doses of
any one individual—even a spouse. That is why is is better for
retirees to continue to compartmentalize their lives to a certain
extent, giving each partner enough space: continuing to cultivate
separate friendships and family relationships and be involved in
activities separate from the spouse. Surprisingly, television is
signaled out as a key reason for senior citizen divorce: if one
partner, now that the career no longer is a factor, becomes a TV
junky and does little more than lie around the house all day,
listening to whatever comes on the tube, the other is likely to lose
respect for that individual—and, as we have already noted, loss of
respect—at *any* age—translates into separation or divorce.

The significance is obvious: it means that, as long as we live
and breathe, we are never home free. We cease growth and
creativity only at great peril.

✦ ✦ ✦

In spite of all our brave words, in spite of all that we can do to
hold off the inevitable, it comes anyhow. The strongest of us only
holds the enemy at bay a little longer—but that "little longer"
represents the difference between pygmies and titans.

Time remorselessly rumbles down the corridors and streets of our lives. But it is not until autumn that most of us become aware that our tickets are stamped with a terminal destination . . . that whatever can be done with our thoughts, words, and actions must be done soon. As we hypnotically watch the steadily diminishing reserve of sand in Life's hourglass, the instincts of a miser surface. Life is now savored, sipped as with a fine nineteenth-century French wine; the years of seasoning now take on distinctiveness. It is during the autumn of our lives that this inner vintage begins to sculpt and paint the face as it seeps through the skin from within.

In the twenties and thirties, external beauty is its own excuse for being, bowling over all who obstruct its path. But, in the fullness of time, the qualities that have become the driving force at last break through into the face and eyes. But this beauty or ugliness of character cannot ever be defined by the same yardstick which we use to measure the beauty of the young. . . . Nemesis sets in: coldness, selfishness, cattiness, vindictiveness, intemperance, harshness, pessimism, gloominess, etc., now are irrevocably and indelibly etched into the muscles of one's face. On the distaff side, warmth, generosity, caring, altruism, temperance, happiness, tenderness, kindness, optimism, etc., now radiate a wonderful glow into the facial muscles, a radiance which becomes ever more pronounced with the passing of the years.

> "Nature's first green is gold,
> Her hardest hue to hold.
> Her early leaf's a flower;
> But only so an hour.
> Then leaf subsides to leaf.
> So Eden sank to grief,
> So dawn goes down to day.
> Nothing gold can stay."

CHAPTER 22

♦

In Conclusion

Even in the stygian moral darkness that blankets our land, each one of us can light a candle, can illuminate with pure light a small corner, thus effecting a new beginning. But regarding this study you may well ask, "Just what is it, specifically, that we can do to change our troubled society for the better? Are there no solutions?"

Certainly, there are.

First and foremost, I am not advocating stepping back into a Stone Age. Like it or not, today we live in an electronic society with cinema, television, videos, radio, etc.—realities that all of us must learn how to relate to, respond to, or help to change. Since I chair a college department that trains media specialists, it is certainly not my objective to denigrate the media. Ironically, however, the students who are most effective, most creative, in terms of their ability to innovate in this field are those, almost without exception, who were shielded from the media as much as possible during the early years of their lives. And the other side of the coin: generally speaking, the more media programming they have been exposed to, the less creative they are, even in terms of media use, advertising, etc.

I have allocated considerable space to creativity, innovativeness, the sense of wonder—qualities we are producing less and less of. People such as my maternal grandfather, Herbert N. Lininger, true originals, are showing up with deeply disturbing rarity today. Without originals our society will continue to degenerate and our standard of living will continue to drop. Just a few days ago an acquaintance who has worked for Montgomery Ward for many years, hearing about this study, remarked, "Like you say, there are all too few originals today. . . . More and more often I hear people complaining about how much trouble it is to make decisions for themselves. They just want someone to take care of them and make the decisions *for* them. . . . It's no wonder we can't compete internationally anymore!"

I have also commented in terms of what has been happening to us ethically and spiritually. We have discovered, in this study, that not only do we have to protect the child and youth in terms of evil, but we as adults remain vulnerable in this respect until our last dying breath.

I am also urging—besides a return to religion and positive values—a return to the family, the family we as a people once had, but have no longer; the marriage for life we once had, but have no longer; the extended family we once had, but have no longer.

"Out of a world of total silence and darkness Helen Keller found a way to a world of light and holy purpose. In the top floor bedroom at Forest Hills where she formerly lived there were eight windows looking out into a vast expanse of blue sky by day and of star-studded velvet by night. Small strings guided her steps to the sanctuary, and there she reveled in an inner illumination that matched the glorious light of day she could not see and the silver sheen of stars she could only feel. She said, 'I learned that it is possible for us to create light and sound and order within us, no matter what calamity may befall us in the outer world' " (Harry Moyle Tippett, Live Happier, p. 8).

At the root of the entire study is the cradle-to-the-grave loss of wonder, the regaining of which ought to be our highest national priority, hence my coda: "The Springs of Wonder."

CHAPTER 23

The Springs of Wonder

Deep within each of us is a spring-watered Eden. So well is it hidden—and so remote is its location—that not even neurosurgeons have been able to find it. No one ever will, for the Creator has declared this glade off-limits to all but one: the owner of the springs.

So it has been, down through the centuries and millenniums, that no matter how great a hell or holocaust one might be compelled to endure . . . always, deep within, there has been that misty glen to escape to and from it to draw sufficient strength and courage and fortitude to enable one to cope with the storms without. Always in this inner Shangri-la there is renewing peace.

But greater even than the gift of peace are the springs that feed these crystal-clear pools. And each spring is a divine miracle of complexity.

How to explain it. Let's see. . . . Well, first of all: No two springs are—or ever have been—exactly the same, just as no two snowflakes are ever exactly alike.

You ask, *What is in the spring water?*

Quite simply, the most powerful substance in the universe: growth—usually appearing as questions. In fact, these springs never provide answers. They only provide questions that can lead to answers. You see, the Creator programmed each of us in His own image, with an insatiable curiosity that, on a much smaller scale, mirrors His. We are like Him in another respect—we are truly happy only when we are growing, when we are learning, when we are becoming.

Do you mean to say that this springwater contains only questions?

Certainly that would be true—initially.

Explain, please.

Well, when infants or very small children go there, questions are about all they draw out.

I can certainly understand that! At that age, they have precious few answers to anything—only questions. But what about when they get older? Don't the springs later on start providing solutions or answers instead?

No . . . not unless the springs become polluted.

You've lost me again.

For this one there are no simple answers. Please listen carefully as I try to explain. It's this way. The Creator is really not interested in anything but growth, and He never measures it against anyone else's, only by the owner of the springs.

I guess it's time to take you to an even more inaccessible spot than the springs: their source. Well, not take you—not even the owner of the springs will ever see that inner sanctum. Only God knows the secret of entry.

You make it sound so mysterious. What happens there at . . . the source?

I'm getting there. Please bear with me. The source, as it has been explained to me, is fed by an astral stream from Heaven itself. It's the purest water in the universe, and every infant has it in undiluted purity. In essence, it represents all the creativity, all the sense of wonder, children are known for. Just how important it is to our Lord was vividly brought home during His earthly ministry when He told His listeners that except as they became as little children again, they would never be in the kingdom with Him and the Father. And to be as a child quite simply means to be filled again with undiluted wonder about life and to seek answers, to seek solutions, to seek out more complex problems and try to solve them, to be forever exploring new roads, empathizing with Robert Frost who, standing at a crossroads, regrets the fact that time is so limited during our brief span of years on this planet that it is impossible to explore everything.

"Two roads diverged in a yellow wood,
And sorry I could not travel both
And be one traveler, long I stood
And looked down one as far as I could
To where it bent in the undergrowth.
. . .

"And both that morning equally lay
In leaves no step had trodden black.
Oh, I kept the first for another day!
Yet knowing how way leads on to way,
I doubted if I should ever come back"
("The Road Not Taken," Robert Frost)

Yes, I agree with you. But where does polluting come in?

Before I get to the pollution factor, I must first explain the natural order of things, the divinely ordained scenario. First of all, I must mention that there is no uniformity of springs. You may have more of them than I.

What?

Do you remember Christ's parable of the talents?

Yes, of course.

Well, you will recall that the recipients weren't entrusted with the same number: one had five, one two, and one poor unfortunate had only one. Since we are each created uniquely different, our talents will reflect this. Hence, some may be blessed—or cursed, depending on their viewpoint—by having their Edenic pools fed by five or more springs, others four, three, two, or just one. But when it's just one, it is invariably a big one. After all, the Creator is always fair. Each one receives the same amount of creative springwater. For some it is more diffused; for some it is not. I can really identify with the one who was entrusted with five talents: I have so many springs (literature, music, art, writing, travel, people, mentoring/teaching, entrepreneurship, popular culture, etc.) that I have always had a mighty difficult time achieving focus. Sometimes I envy those whose pools are fed by one spring only, and who can thus pour all their energies into that one area—be it computers, be it design, be it preaching, be it horticulture . . .or whatever.

It is in the order of things that these pools be continually drawn from, be used. If they are not, they inevitably will become polluted and stagnant, and all the lush vegetation that makes of the spring-fed glen a paradise will lose its vibrant colors and begin to wither—eventually it may die. When that occurs, the owner of the springs will cease to come there at all. At that stage only a miracle could restore the glen to what it once was—well, close to what it once was. Once the springs have been clogged, they will never again flow with their original vibrancy and strength.

But always there are reasons for nonuse of these springs. Reasons the source itself will be come polluted.

How can that happen?

Easy. All too easy. Perhaps this would be a good time to explain how the source is fed. The source always remains a composite force: part divine, part human. As long as the life is lived reasonably in tune with the divine, the elixir flowing from the source to the springs will remain sparkling and clear, the divine compounding the power of the human, the human continuing to provide the questions that result in creative expression and growth.

But if other streams begin to feed in to the source—other streams, which represent thought patterns at variance with the divine—from that time on the springs will begin to sour, the waters will become polluted, and the vegetation will decay.

The source, you see, is, in a way, a mixing chamber, and what is contained therein colors whatever flows through to the springs. It is fed by more than just the divine stream. One stream flows in from the eyes, one from the ears, one from the nose, one from the tongue, and one from the skin. When one reads, the flow occurs as part of the creative growth process—the abstract words being transubstantiated into imagery, imagery unique to the owner of the springs. But not so with imagery that has been created by someone else and then blasted straight into the brain of the springs' owner. Such full-blown prefab imagery represents an alien force, because the owner of the springs has had nothing to do with its creation. As a result, when it flows down from the brain into the source's mixing chamber, it—like oil and water—will refuse to amalgamate . . . and will thereafter proceed on to the springs as a miniature oil spill, beginning there its work of breaking down the once-pure flow. If this prefab imagery—be it of cinema or of television—also embodies a value system at odds with the Creator's, that corrosive element will accelerate the pollution at the source and in the spring-fed pools.

As time passes—days, weeks, months, and years—and the media becomes the key source of "energy" flowing in, the inner process of pollution, stagnation, and decay will pick up speed. Long before this point the poisoning of these springs of wonder will have inevitably and inexorably resulted in the poisoning, souring, and premature aging of the owner of the springs.

Whatever is fed into the senses quickly flows into the source: family wrangling, parental counsel or condemnation, walks in the forest or on the seashore, classroom instruction, sermons from the pulpit and by example, the fragrance of roses in a garden, satanic violence in heavy metal videos, an amoral sitcom on TV, an obscene film in a theater, conversation with a dear friend, the reading of a good book, helping an old man across a busy street, a hymn of redemption, drug or other substance-abuse highs and lows, sexual experiences (both actual and vicarious), dialogue (clean as well as foul) heard and participated in, symphony concert or play, prayer and devotion, hobby growth and fulfillment, travel to new places, making a new friend and deepening the relationship with an old one, writing a bitter letter, swearing at someone, ridiculing a child—each and all has an effect further down the line either for good or for evil. Tennyson recognized this when he said in *Ulysses*: "I am a part of all that I have met."

If the sense of wonder continues to flower, eventually the world will recognize a Leonardo da Vinci, a Martin Luther, a John Wesley, a Leo Tolstoy, an Emily Dickinson, a Helen Keller, a Thomas Edison. But if the dark power becomes the principal energy source, the inner springs will sour, will curdle, will stain everything they touch, and the world will recognize an Adolf Hitler, a Delilah, a Herodias, a Caligula, a Joseph Stalin.

The difference between the two is no farther away than your TV remote control.

✦ ✦ ✦

This book started out being a book about the media; it ended up being a book about life itself.